ACTING LESSONS
FOR LIVING

PLAY THE SCENES OF YOUR LIFE WITH
INTENTION, PRESENCE AND PURE POTENTIAL

*Live your Life's Play
with Zest and
take a Bow!*

Ruthie Landis

ACTING LESSONS FOR LIVING

PLAY THE SCENES OF YOUR LIFE WITH INTENTION, PRESENCE AND PURE POTENTIAL

A LIVING, ACTING AND ENNEAGRAM MASTER CLASS

RUTHIE LANDIS

author of the #1 best-selling book
BEYOND THE BOOKCLUB:
WE ARE THE BOOKS WE MUST READ

ACTING LESSONS FOR LIVING: PLAY THE SCENES OF YOUR LIFE WITH INTENTION, PRESENCE AND PURE POTENTIAL: A LIVING, ACTING AND ENNEAGRAM MASTER CLASS

Published by Gatekeeper Press
2167 Stringtown Rd, Suite 109
Columbus, OH 43123-2989
www.GatekeeperPress.com

ISBN (paperback): 9781642378313
eISBN: 9781642378320

INSPIRATION

In devotion to and in memory of:

My father, Bernie Landis, a great actor and a great human being, forever my learning companion and dear irreplaceable friend. You deserve a standing ovation for your well-lived life.

Dino Biris, truly a man who walked through his life with intention, presence and tremendous positive impact on each person he encountered.

From left to right, Dino and Bernie

And…

To my teachers, students, and clients who have always kept me true.

THE PLAYBILL

*Please note that I have chosen to move between pronouns throughout the text. I try to alternate genders or provide a gender neutral pronoun when possible.

FOREWORD

Ruthie Landis is a visionary, a poet, an actor and a great teacher. She has assisted countless people in achieving a goal of balance and well-being. Drawing on numerous methods and the teachings of many scholars, LANDIS has found ways to interrogate the conflicting forces within us that produce stress and anxiety.

This book will shine a bright light for you on the mystery and marvel of human communication. It will lead the reader on a journey of discovery. It will draw links between what we know and what we imagine. It will offer surprising insights and practices designed to help us find the whole of who we are.

Finding harmony and balance is the goal. Remember, you don't need a guidebook if you know where you're going. But when you don't know where you're going, a guidebook can be a very good thing.

RUTHIE LANDIS is a treasure.

—**Frank Galati**
Tony award winning writer and director,
Oscar nominee, award winning actor,
Professor Emeritus Northwestern University

OPENING CREDITS

INTENTIONALLY BEGIN THIS book with credits. I feel that gratitude is a thread that courses through our time with each other and is perhaps the glue that holds all the threads together of the world I aim to create in these pages. These credits are an integral part of the story I am about to share. They are the backdrop of what is to come. Before the play begins, I always love reading about the actors, director, set and costume designers. This somehow prepares me for the theatrical experience I am going to have. So, take your seat and allow me to share:

I begin by thanking my Life. I want to thank the way my story path has unfolded, though at times I resisted the journey. I want to thank the parts of myself that have **not** resisted and instead followed the energy and led me on. I want to thank the parts of myself that have held intention for a higher good and trusted that whatever presented itself and felt juicy was meant to be explored.

My Life, as it has revealed itself, is not the play-movie that my egoic self thought it would write. And I want to thank my egoic self for stepping aside in pivotal moments, allowing the creative force to decide for me, trusting rather than reacting from fear.

I thank the Cosmic Consciousness that always knew what part I was supposed to play, and what my Essence really wanted to learn in this lifetime. This has guided me and woven the tapestry that is an ever growing and expanding ME.

I bow to and applaud all the characters *within me*, my inner ensemble. They *sometimes* work as a unified cast of characters playing out the scenes of my life with ease, flow, and creative power. I bow to and applaud the *characters within* who sometimes struggle *against* each other, wanting very different things, and thus bring about turmoil for me. When this happens, they play out a lively and tumultuous inner drama.

As I have learned to mine the gold of inner chaos I have discovered a gift that resides in us all. When we really listen to the conflicted parts within us, they teach us how to mediate between them and bring them into alignment as an effective ensemble.

I want to present bouquets of roses to the many cast members who have appeared and will appear in my lifetime. Each person I encounter creates opportunities for me to remove the obstacles between us in creative, and now and then, painful ways. You all can be counted on to play your roles perfectly whether you align or collide with me, whether you feel like my nemesis or my ally. You remind me that this Life of ours is but a play and that finally we all are aspects of Oneness.

I want to thank my grandmothers and grandfathers, my mother and father, my husband, my son, and my brother for intimately co-writing my script and for giving me the opportunity to do lots and lots of rewrites!

I owe so much to my dear friends Joy Becher and Bob Richardson, for sharing with me their profound spiritual journey. They introduced me to the concept of nonduality, with patience. The principles of nonduality have had a huge impact on me and on the writing of this book. You have both taught me well from the inside out.

At Northwestern University I had two very important mentors in the Department of Performance Study, which incorporated acting, directing, and the adaptation of fiction or nonfiction into play form: Frank Galati and the late Dr. Robert S. Breen. Both of these teachers taught me to honor text and excavate subtext, which we will be doing a lot in these pages. I am certain that Frank will recognize many of his familiar teachings as they appear in this book. Both Bob and Frank taught me about point of view (the narrator and camera lens) and how to embody the many aspects of story and character. I am forever indebted to these two amazing scholars, creatives and guides. I wish we three had known the marvelous ancient wisdom of the Enneagram framework of points of view and could have relished in its delights together; but it had not found me yet.

Sets and costume design are critical in all storytelling. My environment informs my writing, and I write best on a cool, clear summer day on my deck in my sacred garden. The trees, the sound of my waterfall, squirrels, birds, butterflies, and the wind all deserve a nod. As for costume design, what does a writer look like? I do choose colors to wear that give support to what I am writing at any given time; so many thanks to my eclectic wardrobe.

In humility, I bow to the teachings of the Enneagram which have infused both my personal and professional life. I implore you, my reader, to stay open to its brilliance. I thank the many teachers I have studied with for the last twenty-five years since my dear one, Joy, introduced this magnificent gem to me. I am in gratitude to each author of the many books about the Enneagram; they have brought their unique interpretations of its truths and wisdom. The Enneagram model is an omniscient guide to the identification of our life-scripts and our potential rewrites.

In every theatrical stage or film production there are those who work behind the scenes. These unseen players impact the quality of the storytelling in innumerable ways. There would be no story-world without them. At the end of a film, the credits move so quickly that all one can absorb is the concept that so many talented people have made this experience happen. In the theatre we call these people the "techies." They were always my favorite people to know and work with, the unsung heroes.

In the writing of this book I, too, have my techie heroes. I sing them a song of gratitude. Shari Stauch, my marketer, motivator, accountability partner, proofreader, promoting me and my last book, always working behind the scenes. Shari, do you hear the thunderous clapping?

For Kathryn O'Day, my patient editor and teacher, I sing a song of praise for her gentle and insightful feedback, schooling me in better storytelling techniques.

I sing a grateful melody to Annalee Letchinger for her insightful and nuanced proof-reading, editing and suggestions. Someday I will finally understand those commas.

And for my husband, Ed, I need to sing you more than a song. You always stand by me and believe in me, even when I don't always believe in me. You have known me in almost all the roles I have played on stage and in life, including the frustrated, hysterical, overwhelmed computer fool I can become. You sit with me and try to ground me in these times of technical hell. You engage in provocative and intense dialogue about each chapter I write and discuss how it can be clearer and even more intentional. You *get me*. You are my critic, editor, and fan. You help me in countless ways I don't always acknowledge. So for the moment, please let the spotlight shine brightly upon *you*, Ed.

And last, but certainly not least, I give my final bow to YOU, my reader. You are the most important character in this particular play of my life where I have been cast in the lead role of author, because it is through you that this unique story will or will not have its run.

My hope is that this book will engage you, change you, and support you in playing the scenes of your own life with crystal clear intention, full presence, and a finale that will knock your socks off.

INTRODUCING...

A LLOW ME TO introduce myself and tell you the story of how I
came to write this play-book. Since we are going to be sharing
time together (with me having lots of stage time as your author
and guide) it's appropriate that you get to know me a bit. It is my hope
that by the end of our time together you will also know yourself in ways
you had not expected.

I wrote this book to help illuminate who we *really* are. By we, I mean
both of us –you and me– because my story is your story. I am using the
metaphor of the theatrical experience to help us see how you and I play
out our lives. My psycho-spiritual experience and my personal stories
will inform us along the way.

From the time I was a small child I was fascinated with why people

behave the way they do, and I was curious about what drove these behaviors. I would ask my Grandma Golde to tell me stories about herself and my grandfather—how they met, what her childhood was like and about previous generations, her own parents and grandparents. I wanted to know all the particulars because I felt these details gave me important information about who I was, too. Then I would make Grandma tell me all the stories she could remember about my mom and dad. Their stories, after all, were the beginnings of my story.

Interviewing my grandma was only the beginning. Even at four years old I would change my clothes many times a day, depending on my mood. My clothes were my costumes—they still are. And, during nap time, my mother would hear lots of noise. It was me moving my furniture around. This was my stage set and I grew bored with it often. I had to keep redesigning the set.

I'm still like that.

My father struggled to support our family by selling shoes, but his passion and true vocation was acting. He saw some potential in me, so by the time I was eight years old he would get us gigs as an acting team. We split the proceeds. He was tough on me and had high standards, and I claimed those gifts and developed them. I was a good actor and I thought that would be my path.

Fast forward to age eighteen, I earned a full scholarship to Northwestern University in the Theatre Department. But I took lots of psychology classes because my real interest was in what made us who we are as human-actors. The University tried to help me create a psycho-drama degree, but in time I chose to major in performance studies for both my undergraduate and graduate degrees. I always seemed to have the capacity to see the unseen, to know what was underneath the masks that people lived their lives behind. While I was still in school, I landed an agent who believed in me. I began getting commercials, and I did my first professional, union show. I also started teaching acting, adapting texts and directing, all of which I was passionate about.

Over the next few years I married, became a successful professional working actor and director in Chicago, and a respected acting teacher. I also gave birth to my son, Sasha. During this time, I always tried to be innovative in my acting classes, not only teaching my students to be good actors, but whole people as well. And to help actors with performance anxiety and rejection, I trained to become a body-centered psychotherapist.

Before long, my private practice grew to expand beyond the artistic community. And as they say, "the rest is history."

At a certain juncture I had to choose to focus on one path, and I chose to follow where I believed I had been led all along. I had found my true vocation: I would be a teacher, a guide, and an illuminator, facilitating personal growth one-on-one with clients and in workshop settings.

My actor-self joined together with my psycho-spiritual explorer-self. I integrated the wisdom of the body, various therapeutic frameworks, the Enneagram system of points of view, spirituality, creativity, energy work, and the support of nature. I have given many workshops and Master Classes combining these paradigms.

So, when someone asks me, "How long have you been working on this book?" I answer with honesty, "My whole life."

A key character in my drama is the Enneagram. Before introducing this principle character, let me first familiarize you with the concept behind it. At its most basic, the Enneagram is an ancient teaching around nine personality styles and their relationships with each other. It is a rich and practical tool for recognizing the lens through which we as individuals each view the world. It helps us to recognize that our point of view is not the only point of view.

Throughout these pages the Enneagram will appear, then disappear behind the scenes, then reappear, like a mysterious and powerful character in a play.

So please, let me now give you your first glimpse of this very important guide in my life. Let's meet the Enneagram's cast of characters.

The Enneagram Cast Members

These cast members show up throughout the play of our lives, outside of us and inside of us. Please forgive that their names are numbers. They are each complex, multi-dimensional characters, so I do not want to limit them to a single role or name. Instead I am choosing to give them numbers, as do many experts in the field. Names may be associated with gender, culture, age, or any other limitation.

See if you recognize any of these personality types within you. Pretend you are watching a movie or play and you spot an actor that you know.

#1

One appears in your play in the roles of Improver, Righter of Wrongs, Evaluator and Striver for the Highest Good. **One** is respected by his fellow critics as the person who tries the hardest to make the production as close to perfection as is humanly possible.

#2

Two is usually cast as a supporting character in your play. She plays The Giver, The Unrequited Lover, and The Listener. She can often be noticed behind the scenes, helping in whatever way she can, illuminating and anticipating needs. She works very hard to orchestrate things and keep the production moving along, trying to keep all concerned as happy as she can. One day she hopes to have a starring role as The Mutual Lover.

#3

Audience members will recognize **Three** immediately in your play. She lights up the stage, is always well prepared, and has been recognized for her many accomplishments onstage and off.

Three has had the courage to get herself *out there* when other cast members may hesitate to be bold. She always reminds the cast "The show must go on!" She is usually The Star of your production.

#4

Four brings depth, drama and meaning to your story. He makes your story memorable and unforgettable. He has appeared as Outlier, Unicorn, Deep-Sea Diver, and The Romantic Creative. **Four** reminds all other cast members to be believable and to play honestly from their hearts.

#5

Five is cast in many roles in your play including Mr. Enigma, The Mime, The Wise Fool, (as in Shakespeare's plays) and The Witness. He has been known to be the director's secret chief consultant and expert script excavator. He remains one of the most mysterious cast members. He is a man of few words, unless he has something important to teach and then his sage-like verbosity is exquisite.

#6

Six appears in your play sometimes as The Antagonist (a much-needed cast member), and also plays the roles of Detective, Provocateur, Inquisitor, and Loyal Friend. Six holds the ensemble together like a tribe and makes sure everyone in the play is comfortable. Six has a great sense of humor, is funny herself, and laughs wholeheartedly at the ironic and comedic scenes in your story.

#7

Seven appears throughout your play as The Adventurer, Visionary, Juggler, Weaver of Possibilities, and Bringer of Sunshine. Seven is happy to be either downstage in front or backstage, just as long as he is kept busy. He does not like to be bored or emotionally uncomfortable so he likes to hang out with Six, Two, and Nine. **Seven** keeps all the balls of the show in the air.

#8

Eight often plays The Leader or The Antagonist in your play. **Eight** plays The Warrior, Protector, CEO, and Mover and Shaker. **Eight** drives the action of your play, creates tension where the drama needs it, and often is either cast as or stands in for The Director. She tends to be blunt and outspoken about what is fair. She also is certain her way is the best way.

#9

Nine is an underrated actor in your play. He has played The Invisible Man, Gandhi, The Peaceful Immovable Boulder, and is The Choral Director of the company who facilitates the ensemble to sing in beautiful harmony. When he comes from behind the curtain for his bow, it is impossible not to notice his power and his strength.

I invite you to begin thinking about these roles and which of them feel most familiar to you. There's no need to choose a single one at this point. Keep an open mind and notice if you have ever cast yourself in any of these roles.

And now onto the Hero's Journey that we each take in our lives.

HERO'S JOURNEY

I RECENTLY ATTENDED A memorial service for my dear friend, Art. I met Art because he was the overseer, complete support staff, and so much more for my doctor and friend, Chris. The celebration of Art's life lasted more than two hours and the time flew by. People were encouraged to tell stories about Art, and I laughed and cried and nodded in agreement as I resonated with each vivid perception and experience many shared about him. I wanted to stay in the church and continue to learn so much more about this extraordinary man.

Through all these stories one could see that Art had led an authentic life, consistent with his very own personal and moral values. He had been intentional, present, and took actions to manifest what he truly deemed important.

At one point in the service someone invited us to applaud Art. He received an over-the-top standing ovation. And then, later in the service, someone else extended the request for us to stand and applaud his elderly, infirm but strong and devoted mother, who had barely left his side in the last few months of his battle with cancer. The applause for both of them was vigorous and moving. Art, in his alive human form, might have been embarrassed at this attention (he had kept so many of his accomplishments and achievements private), and yet I intuit he would also have felt pleased with being seen and known. His mother, a religious and spiritual woman, the widow of a pastor, was dignified and gracious in her reception of the applause. Everyone attending was happy to have the opportunity to acknowledge such well-lived lives in this way.

I suspect that many people, even very humble ones, would like to be able to feel that they would, at the very least, earn a private, metaphoric bow at the end of their own lives. Not for the adoration or validation necessarily, but for the sense that their lives had been impactful and meaningful. There are things that drive each of us on our journey to the grave, and it would be satisfying to know we had grown toward, and possibly attained, what we truly valued most, with few regrets along the way.

I once gave a workshop called "Finding Our Way Home" with the late author and artist Elizabeth Wagele, using stories and cartoons from her book *The Enneagram of Death*. We combined experiential learning, intellectual inquiry, and music with theatrical readings drawn from a sampling of people with different core Enneagram styles. The inspiring accuracy of the ancient Enneagram model brought participants immediately to their own truths and values around living and dying.

In our workshop each participant unpacked what was important to them and how they viewed their inevitable final Curtain Call. They began to see that the prospect of death informed and affected how they lived their daily life-play. We travel through life with death hovering in the background. The mundane becomes vital. Every conscious or unconscious decision we make has the implication that death is around the corner, though we may not realize this. Actors know they must play each scene as if it is a life or death matter. Most people prefer to avoid thinking about death, yet the certain reality of it remains present for all of us. There will be an end to our play, a finale, our own curtain call.

During the workshop, actors who had portrayed the stories from Elizabeth's book each explored their Enneagram type. I interviewed them, asking them to share their own stories about what they hoped they would leave behind at the end of their lives, their legacies. At this point actor and character converged. Whatever their core Enneagram number or ego structure, actor and character each seemed to want their lives to have meant something to others, and to feel they lived according to their perceived purpose and values.

We human-actors innately want to leave behind our imprint for this fleeting life of ours, to be remembered, to offer our embodied values as a legacy.

Why does an audience sometimes give a standing ovation in the theatre? Not many people pay the plumber and then give him or her applause, even if the service was splendid and the plumber has played his role perfectly. What is it that makes so many people enamored with actors or acting? What makes them willing to give adulation to an actor who plays the role of a plumber in a play or film brilliantly, but not give the same to the plumber who actually repaired their broken toilet?

Perhaps it is because the theatrical art form helps us elevate our lives into a special and transcendent realm. It seems like a world of magic and miracles. Something spiritual is happening when the Creative Force is engaged in this way, and characters in plays, novels, and films have touched into immortality.

People ask me all the time if I miss being an actor as my present profession. The truth is I have never stopped acting. I have integrated acting techniques with everything else I do personally and professionally. I sometimes post something on social media from the *old days*—commercials I'd performed in or newspaper articles written about me. It amuses me that those are the posts that seem to get the most interest and response. I put so much effort into writing about human nature and personal realization in my real off-stage life, yet these blogs generate fewer comments about what I deem as *more important* work. Many of us are drawn to a theatrical story which is both entertaining and informative because doing our inner work seems like less fun.

Something about ritualizing the human experience, impersonating it believably, instills a sense of awe for so many people. It delights us to visit these worlds of imagination and possibilities. I have always found this fascinating; maybe it's what attracted me to the theatre in the first place. Acting was a way to experience life intensely, to be and do things I might never be or do. And my gifts and skills revealed to me the many dimensions and illuminations of that art form. I could enact and arouse qualities in myself and give them air and space, beyond what I might allow myself to do as Ruthie. Delving into the history and the psyche of a character was the most delicious part, and it remains so in my professional life as a therapist, coach, and teacher of human-actors.

We are all actors.

Many great spiritual teachers know this fact and teach it.

Shakespeare knew it.

Therapists know it and often therapeutically invite clients to create a new narrative for themselves if they are suffering, to reframe the perception of their life story, expanding beyond the confinements of their old narrative. In fact, as a therapist/coach I often work with a client or a couple or a family on practicing new scripts. I frequently hear, "But I can't say that! That's not who I am!"

"Really?" I respond. "Try it! Just try it! Pretend that who you are includes being able to say it, and mean it."

I smile to myself. If I had ever said, "I can't say that line, it's not the character," to a playwright or director, I probably would have been fired. I had to just do it and get behind it fully. And I was always surprised. I was surprised at the freedom it gave me, and how it fleshed out the character in ways I had never imagined possible, because of my own judgments and limiting beliefs about the character and about myself.

As an actor I became aware of ways in which I would limit myself. The characters I played taught me how to liberate myself from these shackles.

I was once in a play called *the Dick Gibson Show,* brilliantly directed by the writer, adaptor, teacher, actor and director, Frank Galati. I was playing the role of a charm school director, Pepper Steep, who helps a sweet, clumsy, awkward but a genius of a young man, Arnold Menchman, transform into someone confident, graceful and "lithe as a cat burglar."

Pepper helps him, but because of his purely physical transformation, he loses his soul. His external metamorphosis and image-change leads to his losing his heart and essence as a human being. This is devastating to my Pepper—a true failure in her eyes, a tragic loss. She believed in Arnold and thought she loved the amazing gifts he carried underneath his klutzy exterior. He appeared to be a *mensch,* a person of integrity and kindness, but he was now "the light that failed."

On the surface, Pepper seemed like a superficial person, only focused on making people and herself *look* good. But what she really wanted was to help people be more of themselves, not less. No coincidence, Pepper and I share this desire.

Frank directed me to ascend a staircase, with a heavenly spotlight on me, during Pepper's vulnerable, heartfelt, closing monologue. Pepper had failed to bring out what was most important for Arnold, to be his purely authentic self. Her Arnold had now disappeared and she was distraught. Frank wanted me to deliver this exposing, and beyond tender speech as if it were an aria from an opera. In fact, glorious music played in the background as I spoke. I argued with Frank; I said Pepper would never do that. I was a young actor, naïve, foolish, and too serious. The truth is that I, Ruthie, didn't *want* to do it, to expose *myself* and be so vulnerable in such a grand way.

This is a perfect example of a limitation I imposed on my character and on myself. Of course, Frank stood his ground. He insisted I had to find, in myself, the capacity to give Pepper this aggrandized moment of courageous transparency. In doing so Pepper fully emerged, and I believe so did I.

From a spiritual point of view, there was no accident that Pepper (the fictitious character) and I (the actor) converged at that moment of my life, and that we truly became friends and mutual teachers for each other. We were one.

My own growth has continued to be around visibility, and I am just now, at a much later Act in my life, embracing it more. I am a spiritual warrior who believes the truth sets you free, that vulnerability and honesty are our greatest strengths, and are the path to living from a more genuine and awakened place. I think of Pepper from time to time and how she helped me expand myself. She was full of vanity and pride, as am I. And she had a big, loving heart, as do I.

In the best of theatrical work, the writer allows the character their true Hero's Journey. This is a term psychoanalyst Carl Jung and author Joseph Campbell used to describe the universal condition that each of us experiences: the adventure which we call life. We struggle through our fixations and strive to come out on the other side of our misguided beliefs about ourselves. The inner and outer struggles and conflicts create the very tension that enthralls us to watch these stories unfold in the theatre.

As audience members, we know these very wars within ourselves. We notice that there really aren't too many plays about the Dalai Lama, or any already enlightened beings. We are much more drawn to witness the human condition at its worst, and that the conclusion manifests with some epiphany. Pepper Steep lost her love, but in the end, she gained her realization; she saw that if you only change on the outside and neglect your personal inner work it will be an empty transformation.

To help others undergo meaningful transformation I teach them a lot about the Enneagram because it develops awareness and empathy, as well as providing a map toward self-mastery. The Enneagram is a vivid and uncanny guiding tool that reveals what already lives in all of us. One doesn't need to be a scholar of the Enneagram to use it well, because you already are you. The Enneagram merely uncovers the perceptions and motivations that drive us.

My father, Bernie Landis, used the Enneagram to achieve self-mastery. He appears on the cover of this book, taking a bow in a production of "Cabaret" that he starred in with Billy Crystal. His eyes are closed in self-reflection, satisfaction and humility. I chose this photo because I feel that my dad had earned the right to take a big bow at the end of his life, like my friend Art. They both worked at playing the scenes of their lives, consciously. Bernie never stopped working on himself, up until the very end.

Bernie also played the role of King Lear, which taught him some important lessons about living and dying. Lear's foolish pride made him betray his most beloved and devoted daughter, because she spoke the truth to him, a truth he did not want to hear. At the end of the play the old infirm monarch, through a haze of diminished capacity, finally breaks free of his pride and his misguided ego and sees what he has done and the poor choices that he has made. He tries to make amends, though too late, as his precious daughter dies. The role of King Lear was a pivotal role for Bernie that made a big difference in how he lived his own life and how he approached his own death.

My father and I worked together on this final scene in King Lear in a class setting. He played Lear brilliantly. My dad learned from Lear and committed himself to self-examination daily and resolved not to wait until it was too late to acknowledge his mistakes, take ownership and grow. He held a consistent intention to see himself more clearly and honestly. And then, in *his* final scene, he went a step even further; he embraced, with acceptance, his *whole* human self. He was determined to live each moment more intentionally, present until his last breath. This is another example of how actor and character meet and grow together.

As individuals traveling through our own Hero's Journey, we may ask ourselves, "How will it end for me?" My father may have died of cancer, but there was no tragedy there. When I asked him on his last day of life if there was anything left for him to do or know, his reply was, "I have finally learned how to truly love and feel loved. What more is there to do?"

I hope that this book helps you identify what role/s you have been playing. I hope it provides skills for discovering what is underneath the masks you wear, your secrets, and how you can live your Hero's Journey and go after what it is you **truly** want, at the deepest level, honestly and openly. This book aspires to show you how the actor's tool chest, in partnership with the Enneagram and other psycho-spiritual teachings, gives you the means to access authenticity and presence. It aims to help you set yourself free from limiting beliefs about *who* you *think* you are.

My wish for you is that reading these words enables you to rewrite any scripts that thwart you from claiming your pure potential, scripts that keep you from living life at a higher and kinder vibration. Finally, when all has been integrated and consciously applied, you, too, can feel ready to take the bow you so deserve for a well-lived life.

I invite you to pause and consider what you have noticed about yourself as you have been reading. We exit this chapter as we enter the next and the curtain rises.

AS THE CURTAIN RISES

A BABY IS BORN. Maybe it is you. Maybe it is me. At that moment all kinds of data and pure potential merge. The play begins.

In theatre, the director, writers, producers, costume, lighting and set designers meet to develop the script, writing and rewriting. The production is envisioned. There are rehearsals and all the participants dive into the story of the hero or protagonist and their supporting players, antagonists and allies, and decide and plan how this story is to be told and embodied. Just like in a play or film, for us human-actors there is much that must come together before our opening nights.

Let's imagine some things for the purpose of joining into the story and teachings of this book.

For fun, we might imagine there are similar preparations to your story and mine as there are for mounting a theatrical production. This visualization does not need to align with your own belief systems. Suspend your disbeliefs, if you have any. We are just playing for now.

Just as a seed has the possibility to become the flower or plant that it can grow into, we too are a seed of sorts. Both the seed and the human have DNA which determines certain potentialities. And then there are the contexts and the conditions of the environment that will inform what the seed or human can ultimately become.

Now imagine the human's seed of pure potential is what we will call, in these pages, a soul seed. This soul seed decides to incarnate in a lifetime and play out a certain role. This soul seed courageously hopes it is ready to learn some new things this time around. Maybe on a prior adventure important lessons were not learned so well. Imagine this soul seed meets with other creative collaborators or guides in another dimension who have some inspirational input into this particular hero's tale. This soul seed has a whole set of supposed limits put into place, as every script must have. It will be determined what family of origin the soul seed will be born into, what culture, what astrological configuration is imprinted at the moment of its birth, what personality or Enneagram lens it will have a predisposition towards. It will be decided what body build it will have (coloring, stature, features), what economic and social status it is born into, whether it will be more left brained or right brained, its intelligence, as well as the entire cast of characters that this soul seed will interact with in its life-play. The soul seed is born with a script and its role to play.

So, the critical question now becomes -- how can a human being grow and transform if there is already a script with a beginning, middle and end? Does that mean our outcomes are predetermined? Don't we have free will?

Rather than fall into a bottomless pit of questions around fate and destiny as opposed to self-determination, we will act *as if* there are choices.

Each actor plays a given role differently. Each actor who plays Hamlet or Lady Macbeth comes to their line readings and character realization uniquely. And yet, there *is* a script and storyline that the character is confined to. Each actor is a collaborative and interpretive artist. And so, absolutely, they must *believe* they are making choices in each moment.

This book takes the position of both/and. We are both limited and free simultaneously, as is the actor. We can hold both of these perspectives at the same time. Both are true. The ME (that I think I am) does have choices, *and* the ME is expressing choices made by something even bigger than ME.

As humans we can act *as if* we are the chooser and the doer, while remaining aware that our fates are truly unpredictable. The actor does the same thing. She acts *as if* she is the character she is playing, and she has to commit to that choice or she will seem inauthentic. The human-actor also has to live her life by committing to her choices, acting *as if* she is determining her fate. And yet she doesn't have any clue about what challenges will face her in the bigger script of life.

In Jungian psychology, the *unconscious mind* (which in theater we might refer to as subtext, that which is underneath the line that is being spoken) shares its thought patterns and revelations with beings of the same species. Carl Jung called this the "human collective unconscious." We are all part of one dream which expresses itself through human instincts and various archetypes or familiar and resonant roles.

Jung also described a phenomenon he called synchronicity; things happen that we didn't plan on and yet they are in perfect alignment with exactly what we need in the moment. This speaks to the idea that something bigger than we are is operating behind the scenes.

After working with actors for many years, I came to see an underlying congruence between the actor and the theatrical role they had been cast to play. Clearly their ME appears to have agreed to play the role and needed to for some good reason, as if the fictional creation of the character and the human-actor were connecting in the collective unconscious. I always ask my acting students, "What has this character come to tell you about yourself at this moment in time?" or "Why do you think you have been cast as this specific character right now and what gifts does this character bring to you?"

We, too, are cast in roles, but we rarely ask ourselves these important questions. "Why this? Why now?" For instance, why am I working at a job I hate? Can there be a gift here? Why am I a wife to someone I don't even like? I chose to be with him so what must I need to learn from that choice?

The actor's process, since it mimics life, helps us achieve clarity and provide tools for living a more actualized and transformative life.

Try this experiment: Look at the various roles you play and how you play them. Write them down and list beneath each what they bring to your life. List them all; wife, mother, sister, friend, sales person, volunteer, etc. Prioritize them. Are all of your characters serving you? Which characters are central to your life-play and which are *bit players*? Should any get a bigger role and be given more time and more space? Should some take up less of your energy?

On a more important scale is the overriding character you play in your life. Learn to be curious about how you may have trapped yourself in a character that believes in certain limitations or has unreasonable expectations. Come from the position that you do have some choices around your intentions and your *raison d'être*. By asking these questions, and using some of the actor's skills you can learn to play out the scenes of your life more effectively and with greater satisfaction.

STAGES AND SPIRALS

All the world's a stage,
And all the men and women merely players;
They have their exits and their entrances;
And one man in his time plays many parts,
His acts being seven ages.
Jacques from *As You Like It* by William Shakespeare

E ACH OF US plays various roles in the many stages of our life;
Shakespeare's character Jacques points to seven of them. In
Jacques' version of the play of a long life, there are seven acts.
As the curtain of life rises, in Act I, the hero is helpless. He returns

to helplessness in Act II scene VII. In Jacques soliloquy, each of these stages becomes a character in and of themself, with their own growth trajectory and adventure.

Jacques describes these stages as:

- the helpless infant
- the whining schoolboy
- the emotional lover
- the devoted soldier
- the wise judge
- the old man still in control of his faculties, and
- the extremely aged, returned to a second state of helplessness.

There is perfection in being born helpless. It is a state of pure potential, needing the support of others to survive. There is great power in this vulnerability and helplessness: it enlists others to join in as scene partners from the start. Jacques' seven acts might suggest that we move through life in a circle, returning to where we began; we are born helpless and die helpless. Yet there is significant transformative potential in the helplessness Jacques describes. We must view this helplessness as the great surrender, the ultimate grasping of humility, which is an important revelation for any of us. We can even be empowered in our vulnerability.

I prefer to view the path we are on as a spiral, in which we do indeed circle back to familiar issues and challenges, hopefully learning from them, and in doing so we ascend as well. This ascension can happen for us by grace and good fortune or, if we are dedicated, we develop ourselves and grow.

My mother was the kind of person who would say, "If I want it done right, I will just do it myself!" She wanted to appear fiercely independent, though of course she was not. Then she developed dementia and an amazing series of opportunities presented themselves to her. First, she eventually stopped being afraid most of the time. She was a fear-based type, a Six on the Enneagram and she was proud of it. One day when her mind was crystal clear she told me quite peacefully, "You know, I have forgotten that I am afraid."

I watched my mom learn to receive help by letting others care for her. She chose to do this with dignity because she had no choice but to receive. Her dignity became queenly around her caregivers: a kind, loving, appreciative, and benevolent queen. She gave many around her a purpose. She suffered from aphasia and couldn't grab the right words, so instead she smiled, and glowed, and laughed appropriately, and reached out to hold a hand. Her *helplessness* made her more present than I had ever known her to be, and it was a blessing to be around her. Her dementia gave her that gift. Mom, you get to take a well-deserved bow, too.

The notion of the spiral's ascension is reminiscent of psycho-analyst Carl Jung's Hero's Journey. Every human being travels their path, identifies their quest, encounters obstacles, overcomes them and finally returns to their starting place, bearing the fruits of their discoveries, and ready to begin again on the next quest, confrontation of obstacles, etc. They are no longer exactly the same person when they begin their next round, and their starting point is no longer the same either. Jung's hero exists in a paradigm in which we all have a shadow side and an enlightened side. Part of the Hero's Journey is claiming the wholeness of those polarities: the dragons the hero slays outside of himself are projections of the dragons within. The outside and the inside are one, joined by what Jung describes as the collective unconscious.

Another way of looking at this is found in the Chinese philosophy called Taoism. The Tao is the absolute and coordinating principle underlying the universe. It is the unconditional and unknowable guiding source of human reality. The Taoist holds the belief that there is a harmonious code of being that upholds the natural order of all that is. The Tao illuminates the constant flow and interchange between two energies: the sometimes dark, feminine, emotional energy (yin), and the brighter, fiery, sun-like, masculine energy (yang).

Just in the same way, playing *opposites* is a key element for the actor as he is building a character's persona (personality or mask) and as he plays the role onstage. There must always be these tensions; they are the lifeblood of a multi-dimensional character. The Tao proposes that this movement and the variances between these energies influence the destinies of creatures and things. Great actors recognize both the shadow and the light of the characters they play. They acknowledge how, if the opposites become too out of balance, it may inexorably lead to the character's demise. This exercise in playing with these polarities is how villains can also be likable and heroes good but flawed and even sometimes unlikable.

We humans are not machines that can continuously stay in balance. Instead, we are in a constant shift between yin and yang, darkness and light. We continue on our journey, circling through familiar encounters that challenge us. We slay one dragon and soon synchronicity brings us another similar one. It's not the same one exactly, but it's a similar dragon. We have changed and so have our dragons, if only slightly. This feels to us like a circle but it's not, because each time we go on our quest, challenge our obstacles and learn something new, we have spiraled in an ascending way. However, growth is not always linear. Sometimes we go down to come up; we need to descend to catalyze an even greater ascension.

The Enneagram is one way to identify our inner dragons. It shows us our patterns of thinking, feeling and behaving when these tiresome repetitive blueprints can feel to us like never-ending circles, like a not so *merry*-go-round. We can become trapped and repeat our patterns over and over again, but with awareness, intention, and conscious action we can break out of them and ascend.

And the spiral continues. For a character in a play we may only see the journey as a completion of one of Jacques' stages. For a human-actor a grander spiral is made possible through the passage and survival of many stages. If the hero is on a path devoted to inner exploration, if he wisely learns from his accumulated experience, over time he will ascend his spiral and achieve self-realization.

ENTRANCES AND EXITS

My front door-outside and inside.

"In the pause, life begins." Rumi

I LOVE DOORS AND what they represent to me. When I traveled around Italy, I found myself taking photos of all kinds of magnificent doorways. And gates. Doorways and gates remind me that I am moving from one way of being to another. Crossing a threshold speaks to a momentary ending and a beginning bursting with pure potential.

All entering is leaving as well.

This year I made a vision board of my front door. Rather than replacing the old, metal, paint-peeled door and buying an attractive new one, my husband encouraged me to collage the old one. I did, and the front of my door is now a mosaic of invitations.

Every entrance is an exit, too. We leave things behind and we bring old things with us. Let us pause before entering.

The collage on my door is hard to miss. I invite qualities, attitudes, and manifestations that I would like to welcome into my home: joy, kindness, compassion, and the desire to learn and grow, to name a few. And yes, prosperity is invited in as well. Why not? My clients, family and friends enter here. A newcomer usually seems surprised at this colorful, arty, and intentional doorway. If these visitors pause with awareness, rather than daydreaming or rushing (no judgment here, only observation), their eyes tend to land on some message on the door they are meant to see. Sometimes they will comment on it. Sometimes I observe the word or image as it gets their attention and I inquire about it. Then I try to notice whether something they were attracted to surfaces during our time together. And since we are in a relationship, maybe the thing they noticed was meant for me, too.

On the other side of the door, the inside part, I made a different collage. This collage invites the person who is leaving to take their experience with them out into the world. The images and words on the door encourage this. These images and words remind us as we leave one side and cross over to the other to be more aware. Our new discoveries can solidify and become purposeful now as we move to our next destination.

Pause before exiting. Every exit is an entrance as well. We have changed in ways we may not be aware of and if we pause we can bring those shifts over the threshold into our next encounters.

We **rush** from place to place, from home to car, from train to office, from store to restaurant. Whether we are entering someone else's home, or even turning on our phone (which is also one great BIG DOORWAY), we must take time to be mindful, to pause and mark these transitions with clear intention. We are often lost in our thoughts, unconsciously pushing ahead to *whatever*.

Pause. Become present. The great Sufi poet, Rumi, reminds us of this. In that moment, that breath, that pause, we have the opportunity to connect with ourselves, our bodies, and all that is. Our breath. Our inspiration.

In Samuel Beckett's play *Happy Days,* Winnie and her husband *talk* and *be* for two Acts. In the first Act, Winnie is buried to her waist in a mound of dirt. In the second Act, she is buried from her neck down. Yet Beckett gives the stage direction often: "Pause. Do."

What can she *do*? She can be. She can move from within to without. She can feel herself through and through before she speaks from a thought, a sensation, a mood that has touched her. I think of Christopher Reeves, who like Winnie was buried from his neck down in a body that he couldn't activate. But in this stillness, through many a pause, he was a loving husband, father and friend, and he created an important foundation devoted to curing spinal cord injury. He did a lot that has lived on past his presence in this lifetime, and though he could not move his body, from the pause, he did and moved a great deal.

Pause. Do.

While I was in college, a prominent director saw me in a production at Northwestern. Right after graduation, I received a magical call asking me to replace an actor in the world premiere of *The Water Engine* by David Mamet. I did not have to audition.

William H. Macy and John Mahoney were in that production, among some other very capable actors. I was elated and terrified. This would be my first Equity (professional) show. I was very young and had not crossed the threshold from student stage actor to professional stage actor. I had to play a few different characters, and was in and out through most of the play. I would have only **one** rehearsal with the cast before filling in for the rest of the run, and a few rehearsals alone with the (thank God) wonderful, kind stage manager, Kim Beringer.

An actor prepares. So, on my own I prepared and prepared. Then, when I had my one rehearsal with the famous director and very famous playwright present, the only note I received was "Louder and Faster."

I stood there, shaking, my heart pounding. "Uh huh. Okay…" I said. You see, I was a very *serious* actor having just graduated from a prestigious theatre school, and about to begin graduate school there, and this, I can tell you, was not what I expected. "Louder and Faster," they repeated. And then they left. I never really had any more contact with them again. I was left to work with "Louder and Faster."

I wanted to play the characters believably and if I just pressed my louder and faster button I knew that would not happen for me. How would I serve the production because they stylistically needed louder and faster and serve myself and the characters too? What was I to do *besides* be louder and faster? Then I remembered the pause. I paused before entering. Even back then, I knew this was what I had to do. Before each entrance, I stood offstage, and paused. I became intentional in the pause. I reconnected with what the character was after. And the rest followed, with me doing what I needed to do "Louder and Faster."

I can't say that the work on stage was very satisfying or that I was in any way memorable in my parts. But I was part of an ensemble, telling a good story. I was very fortunate from a professional point of view. I was humbled. I did the job. But the most important thing that came from that experience was that I remembered to practice the pause. Again, and again.

I pause.

I was playing a scene with Gene Hackman in the film *The Package*. It was a good scene, although it was ultimately cut in the final edit. Still, I learned so much that day. I learned more about "Pause. Do." I couldn't understand why Gene Hackman kept asking the director, Andy Davis, to have me say an altered version of most of his lines in the scene, instead of he himself saying the line. I had enough lines. I didn't need his. During a break I asked why he was doing that. He said he was much more interested in developing his nonverbal reactions than reacting with words. Without words, in the pause, we saw more deeply into the character he was playing. Pause. Do.

The Pause is a ritual.

For me, the simple pause is one of the most powerful rituals I can embrace and practice as a human-actor. Without the pause, many a blunder is made. Without this ritual of the pause, unkindness can unintentionally be played out. Without the pause, how does conscious life begin?

For me, ritual means the embodiment of intention through movement and stillness, words and silence, enacted with concentration and commitment. It makes the energetic , intangible realm very tangible and worldly. The theatre is filled with ritual. Ritual repeats, and in repeating, the body, mind, and heart can remember and reclaim what code they are meant to live by. Ritual can be performed by oneself or in community. So can the potent ritual of the pause.

In the ritual of the pause you can ask yourself, "What do I leave behind as I enter this new space, this new moment, and what do I bring with me?"

In the pause you can ask yourself, "What gift would I like to give myself as I cross this threshold?"

There are many books published about daily practices for a better life. They may talk of rituals of meditation, exercises, journaling, dancing, or singing. Jose Stevens, an author, counselor, and shamanic practitioner I have learned so much from, invites us to sing each day and say thank you to every organ, bone, and system in our body as daily rituals. I actually love doing this ritual when I remember to do it. But I have to *pause* to remember to do it.

I pause and ask myself, what gift do I want to give myself as I enter my next scene?

I am asking something of **myself,** not asking anything from someone else. For you**,** as you pause before entering your next scene, the gift you ask from yourself is to be ready to receive an answer to a particular question that you have thus far been blind to. You may want to gift yourself with being more open so that you can be accessible enough to meet a new friend. You may want to give yourself focused energy in order to change a pattern of thinking or behaving. Your gift to yourself may be the possibility of relating differently to someone with whom you have *issues.* All these gifts can begin manifesting in the mighty ritual of the pause.

Before a painter works on canvas, they have to gesso it, unless they buy it already gessoed. Their loss if they do. To gesso a raw canvas is to cover it with a white glue-like compound which makes the paint adhere to the canvas. Preparing the canvas is like a ritual. There is something powerful and sacred when touching and tending to the blank canvas, painting pure white on its surface, connecting energetically to its potential. All pure potential begins in the preparing. In this case, the preparation of the canvas is the ritual and the pause.

Before we plant seeds or flowers in our gardens, we must till the soil, enrich it, have enough water for its rooting, all to ensure the ground is ready to support its growth. So too, the soul seed needs time and intention—it needs the pause.

The inner experience can become the outer experience by merely taking a breath in a pause. Inhale the intention, exhale the manifestation. This is what intention points us toward.

The pause helps us prepare the *receptive field.* A teacher I studied with long ago used that term. We prepare the receptive field.

Before I sit down to write, I have a ritual of preparing the creative field. I ring a Tibetan bowl, open the seven directions, (south, west, north, east, above, below, and within) place specific crystals in front of the computer to bring in a certain *superconscious* frequency, perhaps pull a divination card, or a rune, or get a message from the I-Ching. This organized theatricality reminds me that I am entering a scene with myself and the reader, as well as interacting with the environment that surrounds me as I write. I invite inspiration with reverence, giving myself the proper pause before diving in.

Another example of a pausing ritual that is familiar to us is witnessed when we watch sports. Baseball pitchers pause and ready themselves for the pitch; they prepare before they throw. And actors have rituals as well. Theatre is full of rituals. They are not about superstition, and do not necessarily concern anything religious. Rather, they are about filling the pause before the action with meaningful, grounding, concentrated awareness.

What are your rituals? How often do you incorporate a pause into your life?

Allow me to share another story that reinforced this in me to a very profound degree. Years ago, I worked with a wonderful teacher, Charlotte Selver, who taught a method called Sensory Awareness. She was one hundred years old when I studied with her. She lived until she was one hundred and four, so believe me, there was much benefit to be had from her work and her many, many pauses. There are people who trained under her still doing these Sensory Awareness trainings and I encourage you to experience them if you have the chance.

Before we would stand, or sit, or move, or speak, we had to drop into the "coming to…" realm. "Coming to" had to originate in the pause. Come to standing. Come to walking. Come to sitting. Charlotte Selver, this fragile wisp of a centenarian, somewhat hard of hearing and definitely challenged in her sight, would bellow, "No! **Come to walking!**"

With headphones on to amplify the sound on the floor as we moved, she could hear and sense our automatic approach to whatever we were doing. "Come to standing. Come to walking. Come to sitting."

We practiced this exercise eight hours a day for a week. It was exhausting and frustrating and it exquisitely illuminated how un-present we were. We live our lives like robots, programmed to follow our to-do lists, not slowing down enough to *come to* much of anything we do. Since we are so programmed, maybe we should program in some pauses. We could even use a bell tone on our cell phones periodically. Come to pausing.

"In the pause, life begins."

Let's say that a client of mine has worked on a particular issue during our session, perhaps beginning to change a stagnating and limiting belief about herself or someone else in her life. As she leaves the session, she might pause, restate or reframe that old belief, and request the new budding thought to accompany her out the door, and inform the next scene about to play out in her life.

You may think, "Are you kidding? I don't have time for all those pauses. I barely have time to get done what I need to get done each day." Give the pause a try. I believe we have all the time we need for those pauses. I believe those quiet chosen moments can make tremendous differences in our lives.

In the studio where I see clients, the space is full of bells, chimes, gongs, drums, and Tibetan singing bowls. At the beginning of each of our *scenes* together my clients are invited to ring a bell, or many if they choose. Some ring the same bell each time. Others play a symphony using lots of the available instruments. It doesn't matter; this moment marks the pause that invites us to settle in, to find presence, and to connect with clarity about our intention (or gift) for this session. As they ring the bell, we pause and wait for its vibration to become inaudible. It has to finish its song. We try to never interrupt the bell's voice, calling us to presence. It clears the space from the energy of the stories of previous clients who had last been in the office. It makes room for the new story that is about to be heard and it also gives me the chance to become intentional and connected, and to remind myself to get out of the way and let Presence do the work.

We pause. We breathe. We prepare the receptive field.

For an actor, intention is essential. Pause and consider.

- What does my character want that they don't already have? (Or maybe they actually have it, but just don't know that they do.)
- How would they know if they got what they desire?
- What would be the proof; a behavior, a gesture, or a comment from their scene partner/s that would confirm they had gotten what they wanted?
- What moves them through the scene toward the thing they believe they lack?

How can you apply this to your life? YOUR intention is essential as well:

- What do I want that I don't already have? (Or maybe I have it and don't know it?).
- How would I know if I have realized my desire?
- What would be the proof—a behavior, a gesture, or validation from others—that would confirm I had received/achieved my desire?
- What will move me from here, this scene, toward the thing I desire?

Perhaps you are interviewing for a job. Your intention is to get the job, yet there are so many factors here beyond your control. You may think you are perfect for the job, but they may have someone already in the company that is just as suited. Remember, when we pause and declare our intention, we must ask ourselves to show up in a way that is *in our control*. We are not acting from a neediness, but we are preparing to give ourselves a gift that is attainable. In this way, we can decide that the interview is just about meeting a new person or making a nice connection. That is something we can manifest on our own.

The result of looking at intention in this way is that we end up feeling more satisfied, more empowered, and more at ease. Whether we get the job or not isn't so important. What matters is how we show up for ourselves. And we may be surprised that our interview goes much better, too. In the pause we connect with pure potential.

Now, characters in a play usually aren't so evolved. If they were their story would not be very interesting to us.

In my acting classes I would try to help the actor distinguish between what the character wants, and what the actor wants. The character is always coming from a sense of lacking, of hunger, of longing. This is what makes their story interesting and drives the scene. But the actor, so as not to suffer the subjective preferences of others, the impersonal rejections, can create an intention that is fully realizable for her, by her. Her intention need not come from a sense that something is missing. Her intention can be about claiming what is in her control, from her ability to give to herself without outside interference. And she can remember this pure intention in the pause.

Pause before entering.
Pause before exiting.
Pause before turning the page.

CHARISMA

W E HAVE JUST pondered the concept of consciously pausing before entering and exiting a place or an interaction. If we are intentional in the pause, keeping it in our field of awareness, we can live with more clarity, with purpose, with favorable outcomes, and toward our pure potential. Just as the actor must hold his intention throughout a scene, so must we as we play out the scenes of our lives. We remember our intention in the pause.

Great actors have a kind of sparkle. Their pause is filled with a kind of energy that we might call charisma. To have charisma is to have the capacity to attract, fascinate, and inspire others. You could place two very similar actors, standing perfectly still, doing and saying nothing at all, on opposite sides of a stage, and most likely one of them will draw more attention than the other.

Why is that? These two actors might look strikingly similar, same height and build, both good looking, almost like twins, yet *one* brings forth the audience's curiosity, almost like a magnet. People who have charisma have magnetism. The charismatic actor receives energy from the experience of being, and he transmits that energy right back. You, the audience, can't take your eyes off of him. Actors with charisma appear to have no ambivalence about being there, being seen, or being observed. They may even be joyful about it.

And there is something welcoming and inviting about the honesty of that. You just notice them and are drawn to them. Something of their essence shines through and we recognize that very same essence in ourselves.

I invite you to notice how you respond when I ask you, "Are you a charismatic person?"

Do you want to be seen and heard, or do you want to hide? Do you want to invite people into your humanity? How might your life be different if you could allow that kind of presence to be exuded? Could you be more effective and make more impact? What if you could feel the power of connection to all aspects of yourself and the people you interact with?

My belief is that we all can access this place that is simultaneously transparent and empowered. We can all claim our charisma. We just need to be intentional about it and be honest with ourselves about why we haven't owned it already. And I will give you a few methods to get there.

To be charismatic is not to be confused with being a show off, narcissist or *ham*, though some people can be that as well. We may recognize this in some famous figures. They have charisma but they have less desirable traits, too. This is very visible in show business, the athletic world, and politics. Everyone who has charisma may not have a very developed soul seed. But charisma, in and of itself, is not about "Hey everybody, look at me. Ta da!" It is not about excluding anyone else. In fact, it is very much about inclusion, openness, and encouraging connectivity energetically. It is about being able to claim your time and your space without contracting inward or withholding yourself out of fear. It is about shining your inner light brightly and giving it freely.

When an actor stands on a stage, under a spotlight, *if* she allows her internal light to meet up with the external light shining on her something truly magical and riveting can happen. Are you aware of your internal light and are you conscious and in charge of when you shine it and when you don't?

I have developed a powerful experiment I use with actors, presenters, or people who just have to get up in front of others and speak. I have them stand still and repeat over and over in front of a class, or an imagined audience, **"This is my time and this is my space"** until they really mean it and are fully committed to these words. For many people it is hard to claim their time and their space wholeheartedly. We may want it deep down, as I believe most people do, but we may go about getting it covertly and with unconscious manipulations.

What if we could stake our claim to our time and our space without shame? You can practice this on your own, standing in front of a full-length mirror. When you try this, remember your only audience is yourself. Say and repeat these words aloud many times, **"This is my time and this is my space."** Feel the truth of this from your feet up to the top of your head. Your whole body, mind and heart must get behind these words with conviction, without any ambivalence.

Why are we here, living this life, if not to wholeheartedly claim our time on this earth plane, and the space we can fill with our unique talents? What we *do* with our time and our space is another matter. What we do is informed by morality, values, and whether we allow our old script to be rewritten into a more expansive one.

Years ago I worked with a newscaster who had a blinking problem. She was really very good at her job and wanted to move up to the role of anchor, but the blinking continued to be an issue. This wasn't dry eye that could be fixed with eye drops because it was psychological. She was conflicted about being seen.

I had her try repeating, "This is my time and this is my space." All kinds of things came up for her that dated back to her childhood. In her family, children were to be seen and not heard. She also had a parent who took up all the air in the room. There was no real space for her. If she did speak up, she was criticized and shut down. And so, years later, she chose to be a TV journalist, for the whole world to see. She did this unconsciously to heal her past.

The body never lies. The parts of this newscaster that still felt unsafe about being seen compelled her eyes to play hide and seek with the camera. Now you see me, now you don't. Her body had news for her, that is for sure. After we worked through the fact that she was no longer that little girl, that she had something valuable to say and that it was her birthright to be seen and heard, she realized there was plenty of room for her and not at the expense of others. Her blinking problem diminished greatly, and she rose to become an anchor on the news. Her intention became clearer, she removed an obstacle from long ago, and she manifested her dream.

Sometimes we can access this way of being as if we are flirting. We can flirt romantically and directly. We can even tap into our animal mating instincts if we choose. We can bewitch anyone we want to connect with, even when we are trying to make a new platonic friend. We can emit an energy that says, "See me; you want to connect with me as much I want to connect with you." It's playful flirting and harmless. And it's not self-conscious or inhibited by any ambivalence about being seen. It's a natural animal instinct we are blessed with.

Certainly, we can word play with each other via banter and teasing, but it is this energetic spark that ignites the fire of interest between people. It takes some courage to put ourselves out there in this way. It takes a real desire to get fully behind that energy and visibility, to stake our claim.

This is my Time and This is my Space.

When an actor auditions there is always a seduction at play, but the methods one uses to entice others can look lots of different ways. Sometimes the behavior can even appear disinterested, but this energy toward connectivity still vibrates underneath. You just feel it. We might use the descriptive phrase, *playing hard to get.* Or the seduction can seem *very* interested: the way we smile at someone, the twinkle in our eyes, the desire to see the other and allow the other to see us. This kind of bonding is what brings people together. There is nothing phony or inauthentic about this. It is very human indeed.

You have learned about the pause (as you enter and exit and in between) and how in that moment you can connect to yourself, then decide and stay aware of what you want to give to yourself (your intention) in the scene you are about to play. You have learned about the need to stake your claim of your time and your space, while being inclusive of the people and the world around you. And you have learned about your inner light that you have been blessed with as a human-actor. Anyone can shine their light if they consciously access it first. Remember the old song "This little light of mine, I'm gonna let it shine?" In fact, it is your birthright to shine your light. When you do it is reciprocated in all kinds of magical ways; others are invited to shine their light too, right back at you. Now let's learn how to access your light and how to receive the light of others through presence.

PRESENCE

THE WORD PRESENCE has a few meanings. It can mean being here now, like when the teacher calls out the names of her students: "Present," the student says, raising his hand when his name is called. He might, in fact, *be there* or elsewhere in his mind; he may even be texting on his phone. Presence is akin to our understanding of charisma: standing delightedly and completely in time and space. In the theatre you probably have heard this called stage presence.

Another meaning of Presence is when we feel goosebumps sensing there is a vision, ghost, apparition or spirit nearby. Shakespeare acknowledged this kind of Presence throughout many of his plays. In contemporary spiritual jargon we may use the word Presence to mean God, the Creator, the One, Universal Intelligence, Consciousness itself.

I'd like to consider that we view the Presence we want to retrieve and embrace in ourselves as it is defined in contemporary spiritual language: being here physically, mentally and spiritually, owning our charisma, and tapping into All that is.

How do we access Presence?

First, we begin with the pause. Remember the pause. Pause before entering.

Then, inside of the pause we direct our attention to intentionally calling Presence in. The way I do this myself is to declare: "I am fully present and I continue to point myself committedly in that direction." That means I put all distractions aside and focus on me now. I cannot be wholly present with others if I am not wholly present with myself.

Many of us may have achieved a sense of this Presence through active mindfulness meditation. I say *active* for a reason. When we meditate in stillness, we might be able to quiet our minds and then float into a divine emptiness. Here we have no body, no ego, and feel purely a part of All that Is. That is a delicious place to access either alone or in a group setting. But can we bring that very same Presence into our *active* lives, and throughout the scenes we play each day, with ourselves and others?

Zen Master Thich Nhat Hanh, an international spiritual leader, peace activist, author and poet, writes about this concept of bringing mindfulness and presence into all of our daily actions, even while we wash dishes or take out the garbage. I reread his wise books often to rekindle these intentions in myself when I lose my way.

The fact is that accessing Presence in ourselves is not a transcendent experience, it is a very body-centered human one. We join body, mind and heart as we cross the threshold from automatic busy brain, robotic body and closed down heart to the other side, where Presence lives. On the other side of the threshold our brain is enlivened and curious but not busy or distracted. Our body's senses are heightened; taste, smell, touch, sight, and hearing all become more vivid. The sixth sense, intuition, is activated as well. And finally, our hearts are brave and receptive. It is like moving from living in black and white to high definition technicolor (without drugs). And it is here we realize we are home.

Perhaps you have seen comic renditions of actors preparing before going on stage. They shake their bodies like pups, roll their necks like Regan in "The Exorcist," stick out their tongues, stretch their mouths, make all kinds of sounds from chimpanzee grunts to big sighs to high operatic trills. They look silly.

Why do they do this? Actors realize that their primary instrument of communication and the container of Presence is their bodies. They must prepare the receptive field. They must stretch out and open up the stuck places in order to be able to reach into all aspects of their humanness.

We see dancers and yoga practitioners and people at the gym preparing their bodies to move more freely to perform. Most of us don't pay much attention to our bodies, unless we are in pain and the body is screaming, "Pay attention!"

We must stretch ourselves in many directions: physically, mentally, emotionally, and spiritually if we are to grow as humans.

I invite you to play with this activity to bring forth Presence in yourself:

Begin by sitting quietly with your eyes closed. Really connect with whatever you are sitting on as if it is your best friend. Try feeling its support. Try meeting it with trust. Try leaning into it. Notice whether this is easy or difficult to do. What do you need from yourself to surrender and become intimate with receiving the support that what you are sitting on is offering to you? The acknowledgment of support is key to finding Presence.

Then scan your body. Stay curious without judgment, if you can. If judgment is there, just notice *it. Allow it. It will dissolve if you allow it to be seen.*

I love the word notice. Notice is soft and inquisitive. Notice what is open and what is closed in your body. Don't try to change a thing. Allow it as it is. There is no preference. Closed does not have to be open now. It will find its way to open if it chooses. Notice if a sigh comes when you invite acceptance of things as they are. The big sigh is breath saying Yes to the moment. The big breath comes when something important is seen and acknowledged. No need to breathe in any particular way. You will breathe how you are meant to breathe.

Notice what feels tired, collapsed, or what feels energized. Allow. No preference.

Notice what feels tight, loose, contracted or expanded. No preference. Notice. Allow.

Stay connected to the quality of the sensations. Do not **interpret** *them at this time, if you can resist. Only allow. Stay curious as if you are just neutrally and compassionately observing. Neutrality and compassion are great companions; they do not cancel each other out.*

Notice if what you are sensing in your body becomes interpreted as emotion; if there is an emotion associated with the sensation, just notice it. No preference. Allow.

If you want to give a voice to a part of your body and let it speak to you, follow that. If not, stay in the noticing and allowing. And… if a voice in the back of your neck says, "I feel tense, thwarted, held back," let it speak. Listen. No need to fix a thing. Your observer self might say to your neck if it is so inclined, "I hear you, even as you feel thwarted. I am listening to you."

What has just happened is that you have become fully present with yourself, without judgment, resistance or preference. You have filled the pause with yourself and Presence. You did this through allowing, through having no preference, and consequently all the energy channels have opened. We are here now. We are energetically connected with ourselves, and on some level, in this compassionate neutrality, we are also connected to All That Is, including the collective unconscious.

Now we are going to expand this out to take Presence to others and the world.

Open your eyes softly to move from the inner eye to the outer eye. Let your gaze be non-preferential as well. Notice what you see. Allow. You are just a camera lens taking in the shot, from very, very close-up (within yourself) to wider close-up (now outside of yourself), to medium shot, to long shot. If you start to lose your Presence, close your eyes, reconnect in the pause, and then gently try to include the visual sense again. Become intentional. Say aloud, "I am Presence."

Then say aloud, "This is my time and this my space." Take your hands and let them sculpt the space around you. Ask yourself, "How far do I go in front of myself? How far to the right? How far to the left? How far behind me do I extend, now and into my past? And what about below me? How deep do I go into the earth? How far do my roots burrow? And now, above?" Let your hands touch the space over your head, as it has felt the other directions. Ask yourself, "Where do I begin and where do I end?" You are getting in touch with the size of your Presence as it is in this moment.

Let us see if we can hold Presence as we are inclusive. Imagine now that you include in your field, while holding your time and your space definitively, the whole environment you are in—the walls and furnishings if you are inside, the sky and earth if you are outside. Reconnect to your senses as you hear the sounds, smell the scents, experience the taste in your mouth, make contact through touch and see what you see. Move back and forth between yourself, your time and your space, and the outer world.

Now widen your field even more to include the people you know, the city you live in, the whole world, while staying connected to your time and your space. This grander field of vision will need to engage your imagination. Move back and forth between self and all the rest. Noticing. Allowing. Accepting with neutral compassion.

If Presence starts to leave you, or if you lose your connection with it, close your eyes and find it again. It's waiting for you because it has been there all along.

There is one more piece to this part of the experiment.

*With eyes open or closed, imagine the direction of **within**. As within so without. Inside each cell of your body is a universe, vast and expansive with all the space you need. Breathe in all that infinite space. You have all the time you need. You have all the space you need. And so does everybody else.*

Now again take your hands and sculpt the space around you. How long are you? How wide are you? How deep are you? Are you bigger or smaller than before you began? Most people find that if they hold their Presence, they can include the world, not lose any pieces of themselves, and even find a more expansive and infinite self in Presence.

I invite you to turn on some music and move and dance from this place of Presence. What can you tap into now that you might not have been able to do before? Does movement flow? Has the ego gone for a nap and taken inhibition with her? Can you move with the wind and can the wind and the breath of inspiration move through you?

For the actor, working with Presence is what manifests inspired and inspiring performances. For us human-actors, working *with* Presence and *as* Presence allows us to play the scenes of our lives kindly, inclusively and with pure potential.

PRE-PRODUCTION

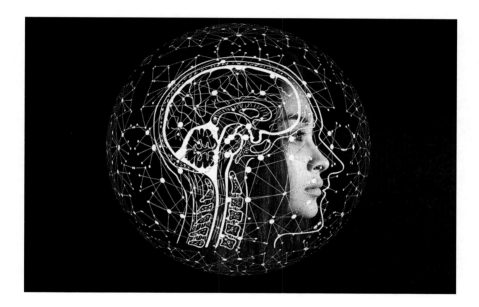

IN A THEATRICAL production, the actor gathers all the possible clues from a script that might help her get to know the character she is playing. She is exploring the **WHO.** She asks herself about the character's family of origin, whether the character felt supported or held back by her family, the culture they were born into, the relationships that she has had in her life thus far in the script, and the victories as well as the traumas she may have experienced.

This creates the back-story for the character. Once this information has been brought into the actor's consciousness, it will never be lost. All this data will inform how she delivers a speech or how she hears a line delivered from her scene partner.

What is your back-story?

Five W's: a chart for the actor and the human-actor to full embodiment

Who am I?	Mask and beneath	Thinking/feeling/behaving patterns
Where am I?	Context/Environment	Triggers and stimulants
What do I want?	Intention	Motivation from a place of lacking
What's in the way?	The Obstacles	Internal and external impediments
What am I going to *do* to get what I want?	The Actions	Strategies and tactics we can use

The five W's are the very same questions I might ask on an intake form I give to a new client. The answers to these questions will help me understand who the client believes they are, and where their strengths and their suffering may be coming from. The Enneagram (which we will continue to learn about as it makes its entrances and exits in this play-book) gives an uncanny snapshot of the stories we tell about ourselves; it helps us identify the patterns we habitually repeat in our thoughts; it helps us spot the feelings that frequently arise in us; and it alerts us to our actions and reactions. That's why I have found the Enneagram to be an essential tool for actors, directors, writers, and **all** people interested in self-development.

If it is important for an actor to know all these things about a character he is trying to play, isn't it equally important for us to access this same knowledge about ourselves? Yet many of us have little or no curiosity around exploring our own narrative, and this lack of interest keeps us from playing ourselves well in our lives. Socrates warned us: "An unexamined life is not worth living."

People these days are paying to test their DNA in order to find out what ethnicities and cultures appear in their blood. Yet these same people may spend very little time looking at their emotional, relational and psycho-spiritual legacies. In my first book, *BEYOND THE BOOKCLUB: WE ARE THE BOOKS WE MUST READ* I explored how we can read ourselves, privately, and in community. In *ACTING LESSONS FOR LIVING* I continue to prioritize self-awareness, only now we are looking at action and implementation. We are the characters we must watch in our own play.

I invite you to pretend you are an actor; the character you are going to play is you. Be curious. Bring forth the director/observer/witness/ audience in yourself as well. Apply the five W's to yourself. These are all the things we take for granted yet they run the show in the background, through our unconscious. We need to bring them into the foreground, into our awareness, so that we may live with more intention and presence, and achieve our potential as compassionate and awake humans.

First, get to know the **WHO** and her back-story in detail and depth. Journal about her. Go through old photographs. Interview relatives and old friends. This is what serious actors do, why not you? How does your observer-self perceive your **WHO**?

I would include in this line of questioning your costumes, too. They very much inform your **WHO**. Costume is part of our persona (mask). Clothing discloses what we choose to show the world about who we think we are or how we want to be perceived. What clothes do you feel most comfortable wearing and what apparel or uniform never feels right? What does that piece of data tell you about yourself and what does it reveal to others?

I have given workshops around this very topic called What's Your Style? During the workshop we explore how our clothing choices are informed by our Enneagram type. We ask ourselves, "How does what I choose to wear grow from who I think I am?" Participants choose fabrics and create a vision board for themselves. They also bring one article of clothing that they have in their closet but which they never wear. We each dialogue with this piece of clothing and wonderful awarenesses are revealed to us. Why do I keep it but won't wear it? Is it something I believe I want to wear but it doesn't fit into my image? Or it no longer fits me...because my size has changed. Does it represent a disowned part of myself?

For an actor, her costume might be the key to unlocking a character; when she puts it on for the first time it is transformative. When I put on a wig as my character and look in the mirror, I feel an immediate shift. When I wear a pair of shoes that belongs to my character, I walk differently. Actor Johnny Depp, known for his quirky characters, has often spoken about the transformative power of costuming. Think about how his costumes for Edward Scissorhands, Willy Wonka, and Captain Jack Sparrow inform his characterizations.

How do your personal "costume" choices inform you? What colors do you like to wear or be around? Do you like wearing make-up and use hair products or prefer *au naturale*? And what does all this tell you about who you think you are? The color brown has never been my favorite, but as I was working on self-expansion, I started to purposefully wear brown, and even bought brown leather couches for my office. I grew to feel comfortable with brown; it grounded me and broke through the limitations of my self-perceptions, what I thought was ME and what wasn't. I gravitate toward vivid and watery colors: turquoise and purple and teal. These colors lift my spirit. But I consciously choose to explore a more varied palette to make myself more complete. In order to expand yourself you must enter the world of the non-habitual, which means moving beyond your comfort zone.

Let's move on to the **WHERE.** This is the external material world you experience. Ask yourself these questions and possibly journal about them:

- What environments do I feel confident and safe in?

- Where do I feel threatened or triggered into reacting defensively?

- What places can I call my territory and claim as my own?
- When I walk into a room where do I choose to sit? Why there?

Now we are engaging in the set design of your life-play. When decorating my home I choose an array of colors that correlate with the chakra system (an ancient map of energy channels). I strategically paint specific rooms in my house with specific colors from the chakra colors: survival/root chakra is red, creative chakra is orange, power chakra is yellow, heart chakra is green, throat chakra is blue, intuitive chakra is indigo, and crown chakra is violet. These colors support those energies and aspects of our whole self. They have a certain vibration. Set and costume designers understand this intuitively. Different colors communicate different things. It is a good thing my husband is somewhat color blind, which makes him very flexible and forgiving in this area of our lives together.

Everywhere you go, you are playing a scene, with all the same ingredients that we observe on stage or film. Only the character in a play rarely comes from a high level of self-awareness. The reason for this is because our entertainment depends on watching them grow into greater awareness...or not. That is what is essential here. You can practice seeing far more about yourself than a character has the capacity to see; in doing so you amplify the possibilities of who you can become, *unlike* the character frozen in his script.

As for the **WHERE,** the environment or the set in a play or film is a critical part of the story telling. I use this knowledge about territory and venue in my studio. When a new client enters my office, I invite them to pause and determine where they want to sit. I have two couches and an armchair, so they have some choices here. One couch faces the door and people who feel nervous may want to keep their eye on that exit. Someone else might choose the couch that faces away from the door and has the best view of the whole room. The room is filled with playful and meaningful objects. Perhaps that client wants to take all that in for a reason. Also, this couch is larger and has the option of *lying down or stretching out,* which might be symbolic of what it is they want to do in our session; they want to feel supported and stretch themselves. And the armchair faces the door as well and there is a feeling of structure, power, and containment when you sit in it.

All of these options are revealing to me about WHO I am meeting. What makes them feel safe? Where do they choose to sit and why there? It is interesting that when I have seen a client for a good while they may choose a different seat. It is time for a new perspective, which means the client is changing.

You can consider these things when you decorate your home or office. They, too, are sets. One aspect of my work with clients can include interior design, especially when they are hoarders, or when they are going through a divorce or loss. Changing their set (their outer world) can greatly impact their inner transformation.

WHERE also includes the lighting. I have many different lighting options in my studio. Some clients do not like the overhead spotlight lighting. It may feel exposing to them or harsh. Others might love it. Some people prefer dimmer, softer lighting and I have made that request easy to accommodate, with different lamps all around the room. Our preferences around lighting are also very telling. In the chapter on Charisma we realized that when we can claim our inner light and shine it freely, the lights outside of us shine right back at us. So the lighting in the room allows us to be seen or not be seen, to shine our light or retreat from it.

There is a whole chapter coming up called **What Do You Really, Really Want?** But for now, before reading what I have to say about that, just ask yourself these questions about **Want**.

- What do I want from this moment?
- What do I want to get from reading this book?
- What do I want from life?
- What motivates and moves me?

This naturally progresses into, **What's in the way of getting what I want?** These are the obstacles within us and outside of us. These are the dragons we slay or tame within our own psyche or that appear as outside challenges. There are many obstacles outside of us that can prevent us from getting what we want: not enough support, enemies, no opportunities, others not recognizing our value. But our *perceptions* of these outer obstacles are truly what hold us back the most from getting what we really want. What holds us back is an inner saboteur, our unconscious resistance to change, our fear of becoming more than who we think we are.

Jot down a few outer obstacles that have kept you from moving forward toward an objective. Then see if you have a corresponding belief about yourself that makes opportunity invisible to you.

What am I going to *do* to get what I want? The very first thing we must *do* to get what we want is to come clean with ourselves around the four other W's. I can make a list of great strategies and tactics to achieve my end goals, but if my obstacles are internal, if I am unconsciously attached to my old narrative, the *to do list* will never get done well or at all. I must tame my inner dragons before I can manifest my desires. And I must get very clear on whether what I want is a futile desire, one that leads to yet more desires. Or is what I want truly for my highest good and in alignment with my life's purpose?

The familiar phrase applies here, "Be careful what you wish for." When I have removed my inner obstacles through honest introspection and by challenging my often misguided thoughts, I can begin to explore how I play out the scenes of my life authentically, truly open to pure potential.

A metaphoric curtain rose the moment you were born. It will symbolically descend at your death. There are many givens that figure into this play of your life. Your soul seed has a course, a Hero's Journey.

Your personal destiny is both in your hands and part of a much bigger production. It is up to you where you put your intention and attention as you go. It is up to you to decide how you play your part.

MY ROLE – WHO AM I?

(The Enneagram enters from stage left)

IN THE EARLIER chapter, **As the Curtain Rises,** we explored how your role began to develop from birth. You were cast as a particular character in the scenes of your childhood, and you were born with tendencies to see and respond to the world in a particular way, with a personality. Perhaps those personality traits were even embedded in your DNA. You became hard wired to take on your very own stereotype.

In fact, you unconsciously agreed to typecast yourself. Even if you constantly *rebelled* against the role you felt you were given, then the *Rebel* became your role. Like it or not, you were stuck and probably unaware of who you were cast to be. What might not have yet been written was who you were meant to become.

As an acting teacher I frequently hear actors complain about the limitations of being typecast. An actor might look a certain way or sound a particular way, and casting directors, directors, and producers immediately put them in a category. From the actor's point of view this doesn't feel fair. After all, they were trained to play *any* role believably, to develop their empathic imagination and step into a character's life. The actors despair and feel frustrated and thwarted.

As awful as this feels to them this is part of the industry they chose. Of course, the director needs to categorize. If you are out shopping for shoes and you see a pair on a shelf you immediately label it in your mind: dress shoe, athletic shoe, beach shoe. You have to be decisive and appropriate about what you are about to buy. Casting an actor is the same process. Many critics will write in a review that a lead actor was mis-cast and he ruined the play or film. So, producers and directors take great care when casting.

The actor may beg their agent to send them out on auditions to stretch themselves and play roles outside their category, but the truth is that unless they have stellar box office credibility, or are VERY lucky, what they yearn for is just not going to happen. The actor may argue that they are a trained and gifted actor, deep, layered and very flexible. They may remind their agent that with lots of makeup and padding they can transform from the waif to the gargoyle. But rarely will that happen. And if the actor wants to work, wants to survive as an actor and not just via their *day job*, they must accept the way they are perceived and even exploit it or leverage it.

In my acting classes or when I work with an actor privately, I interview them and film the interview. I also do this with executives, newscasters, and leaders who are wanting to explore what it is they actually project to the people they encounter. I have often thought that some politicians who struggle with projecting an accessible persona should have done this work. It could make a big difference in whether they win or lose an election.

Then I ask the client to watch the interview of themselves and imagine they had never met the person whose interview they were watching. "Who is that person?" "What are the qualities they exude?" "Are they high status or low status?" "If you would cast them in a role what would that role be?" If the client is being honest with themselves, they are often surprised by their answers. There is an incongruence in how they have previously perceived themselves and what they actually see when they watch their interview. They rarely say, "Oh yeah, that person could be or play anything."

We rarely have an accurate perception of ourselves. It is possible that when a client looks at themself in the mirror, they see what they want to see. I know that when I look in the mirror, I position my face *just so* in a way that I won't have to look at my jowl. I create blind spots around my jawline. Think of all the comedy routines around people taking selfies. Delete. Trash. Delete.

Imagine all the other things I might not want to look at about myself. As we use the Enneagram and the map of insights it can provide for us, we may be able to see ourselves more clearly and even be more accepting.

When I was auditioning for commercials, I remember casting agents or directors saying, "Just be yourself." This always made me laugh inside. *What does that mean?* I am so many things. And though that was certainly true, we are each multidimensional and complex beings, I was projecting *something* in my demeanor, energy or body language. I was making them think I was a certain kind of person, the one they had typed me as, beyond my physical appearance.

I am sure they sensed that I, defaulting to my Two-ish (Giver) behavior, wanted to please them. I was eager, and attentive, and likable. I was engaged and engaging. I rarely challenged them, but rather tried to really understand what it was they wanted. How could I, a shape-shifting Two, transform myself into what they desired? But a Two can easily act like other numbers on the Enneagram model because of their desire to please. If they wanted tough they got tough like an Eight (CEO). If they wanted aloof, they got aloof, like a Five (Mr. Enigma) or a Nine (The Invisible Man).

From their point of view, by defaulting to my Enneagram predisposition to accommodate, as opposed to being my true self, I was "acting" and not "being." I had type-cast myself and didn't realize it.

Though I was a very intelligent, perceptive, and strong young woman, with a full scholarship at Northwestern University, teaching acting in their summer program at only nineteen years old, I was also five foot two, eyes of blue, with curly red hair, a youthful light voice, and a soft demeanor, pretty low-status appearance-wise, at least in the eyes of others. The way I looked and sounded did not necessarily match up with all of who I was within. When I began auditioning professionally, I either had to accept that I would often be cast as the *ditz* and run with it, or not work at all.

So, I embraced the role of "best friend" to the lead, comic airhead, or vulnerable space cadet. I wanted to work and because I didn't resist the stereotypes, I did work—a lot. Still, like my fellow actors, I wanted to be more than I appeared to be. If only I was taller, and less curvy, and had a deeper voice, with angular facial features, I could be the leading lady, or so I thought.

The way around that for myself was to create one-woman shows that allowed me to explore a range of characters beyond how others might have perceived me: Gertrude Stein, Colette, Moll Flanders, Dorothy Parker and others.

Ruthie as Gertrude Stein and as Dorothy Parker

As I reflect on that time now, I see that I have always wanted to expand out from a limiting image, and by meeting up with unlikely characters I could break out of my self-inflicted box. I wanted to tear down the walls of my self-imposed container and be *more*. In fact, I still do. It was one thing to accept those limits in order to land an acting job; it was another thing to believe that the ME that was presenting herself a certain way was the only ME I could be.

That is why each day I remind myself that I alone can release ME from the package I have identified with. And I must be completely conscious about what I have identified with before I can begin to dis-identify with it. When I can own my default patterns of thinking, feeling, and behaving, as well as my motivations, secrets, and lies, then I can make alternative choices and really grow as a person. This is my transformative work.

So now, as you unpack who you think *you* are, with all your strengths and challenges, I invite you to revisit these three questions. They are worth journaling about, too.

- What do I choose to show of myself to the world?

- How do I alter or enhance my image?

- What are the secrets I keep and why do I hide them?

As I have already shared, my father was an actor and a seeker of truth, committed to personal transformation. Besides being part of our father-daughter acting team and learning from him in that way, I was most influenced by his constant reading about human potential and personal healing. So even though we were very different Enneagram types, me a Two, he a Five, we were kindred spirits. We were extremely congruent in our interests (except for sports, which he loved and I grew to tolerate).

When I was in high school, I wrote a short play about an old man in a rocking chair and a precocious little girl on a rocking horse, a lá Samuel Beckett. The two characters rocked back and forth, back and forth, discussing their vulnerabilities, the things they despaired over and longed for, the meaning of life, and what was on the other side of the only door in the room. Perhaps death? I directed my father and myself and we performed it together as a special production.

I wish I had that play now to read again. There was much about it that was premonitory, predicting the quality of the relationship my father and I shared as we continued our journeys together through life, until my father got off his rocking chair (in reality his Lazyboy recliner) and walked through his only exit, to the *other side*. Even as I write this people reminisce about that high school production. The profound soul connection between my father and myself resonated beyond our own relationship.

When I began to teach acting and became a professional actor in Chicago, our roles were reversed and I became my father's acting mentor. When he moved back to Chicago from Ohio, he attended my acting classes and self-development workshops, and hired me for private coaching. We had, as one friend called it, "a remarkable relationship."

When he died there was a full-page obituary in the newspaper headlined, "One of Chicago's Great Actors." He worked at all the major theatres in Chicago, appeared in a long run just off-Broadway, in regional theatres throughout the U.S., and in commercials and films. Yet my father's personal mission was to become a whole integrated human being. I believe he achieved success in that as well. He was honored with the Humanitarian Award at the prestigious Chicago Shakespeare Theatre. My father's obituary could have been headlined, "One of Chicago's Great People."

And this is what I strive for and why I have written this book.

When I was introduced to the Enneagram twenty-five years ago it was as if my dad and I had finally found what we had been searching for. This was a tool that could merge our desire to enhance our acting skills with spiritual and personal growth. Eureka!

The Enneagram gives us a dynamic and complex chart of nine ways of coming to the world, in the same sense that Charlotte Selver, my Sensory Awareness teacher, had taught me to "come to" each moment.

The Enneagram gives us a framework that helps us to identify the vessel we have put ourselves in. Through the Enneagram's framework, we can identify our secrets, what we hide from ourselves and others, and finally, remove our masks to express our true selves.

Some people may at first feel threatened by this model because they interpret it as something that will limit them, or reduce them to a stereotype. This is confusing the mask with the self. The Enneagram teaches us about the mask so we can access our soul. Some people may resist the Enneagram because they feel it can be weaponized against them. I have witnessed this as a workshop participant myself led by less conscious people who fail to understand the Enneagram's true purpose. Any theory or philosophy can be distorted and misused. And so can the Enneagram. This is not the fault of the Enneagram treasure, but rather of the less aware facilitators.

I believe it is worth taking the risk to dive into its wisdom in order to grow. The Enneagram's purpose is to be a guide on our unique Hero's Journey. At its best it allows us to see and be seen in miraculous and useful ways.

Though the Enneagram is complex and dynamic, it is my intention to make it easily accessible to you. Here is a little introduction about how it works:

Enneagram Styles

Enneagram means Drawing of Nine and it is a kind of medicine wheel of sorts, if one uses it that way. We appear to have a dominant style that we default to and other styles that we have developed access to.

The diagram above, consisting of nine numbers arranged clockwise in a circle, represents the Enneagram. The numbers represent our dominant styles or masks. These roles (numbers on the diagram) are organic and we don them unconsciously (more on the numbers later in the chapter).

Each number on the diagram has next door neighbors on either side (Two's neighbors are One and Three, for example). These neighboring numbers are referred to as wings. Wings are energies, motivations and strategies that you can access and might recognize fairly easily.

Of course we all take on different roles at different times, so each number also has arrows to depict the various movements we might take to jump into the worldview of different numbers. Each arrow points us to a different point of view. This has the potential to loosen the grip of over-identifying or over-developing just one way of seeing life. Our uniqueness as individuals is determined by how dynamic and nuanced the movement between the arrows is.

You may also notice that neither the arrows nor wings appear to touch each number. This doesn't mean you can't access them; it means they might be less familiar to you. Each number has teaching potential for each of us whether we access them easily or not.

When I teach an Enneagram for Actors Master Class, I invite each student, for the next nine days, to choose one number each day to walk around in. They have to dress as that number might dress, eat food as that number might eat, and interact with other people in their lives the way that number would. They have to experience their own life through the lens of a different paradigm.

It is always easiest to live through the numbers the actors are most familiar with, their dominant number and their arrows, their already accessible places. The other numbers, however, give them unexpected gifts as they embrace their shadows, or disowned parts. They experience the world very differently as they put on the *glasses* of another type. This is an acting task for them, and *serious* actors take their challenges very seriously.

The actors are not allowed to resort to caricatures. Nor are they allowed to judge their character. As the actors experience these new motivations, thoughts, feelings, and behaviors, pure potential rises in them from these shadow numbers, and something is set free. New ways of being become possible. This activity expands who the actor thought he was, and gives him all kinds of new choices about how he might go about playing his part and living his life.

My father, Bernie, embraced the Enneagram, a fervent convert. He used it to develop every character he played and used it during every audition he went to. Often at an audition, especially for commercials or films, the director will ask the actor, "Can you do it another way? Show me more." Lots of times these scenes are short, maybe only one line. Most actors hear that what the director wants is a different line reading, stressing other words in a speech, making the character bigger, or pulling back and doing less. But this is superficial and inauthentic. It is grasping at straws, faking it, and improvising without a clear motivation.

When a director asked Bernie to show her more, he giggled within and replied, "I'd like to try it nine different ways, if you'll let me."

The director would be startled "Nine?" they'd ask.

Bernie would enthusiastically exclaim, "Trust me!" Then he'd proceed to give nine completely different fully embodied, clearly motivated renditions. It was like nine different people appeared before the director's eyes. You can imagine Bernie landed a lot of those jobs. He did so because he had worked hard to understand and own all the nine Enneagram numbers in himself. He loved playing all nine of them equally and this led to much of his personal growth.

I invite my personal growth clients to experiment in the same way. As I have said, we are all human-actors and we can pretend. If I am in a challenging situation, how would another Enneagram type advise me to perceive the situation? What would it feel like to rehearse a scene in my life, but play it as a number who sees the situation in the opposite way that I do? What new options would be revealed to me?

There are many teachers of the Enneagram with many books and materials, and even different schools and trainings. Each book or seminar is taught from the unique point of view of the author/ facilitator, who has their very own Enneagram perception, personality, and style of communicating. So, you will need to discern which authors/ teachers resonate with you the most, offering you the best way *into* the Enneagram's endless gems and benefits.

It is absolutely worth taking the time and energy to immerse yourself in the Enneagram if you are serious about leading a more conscious and value driven life, full of pure potential. In the Enneagram community there are different philosophies and lineages that teachers come from, just like teachers of Tai Chi or Qigong. Some teachers focus on the Enneagram in career and corporations, some see it as a spiritual model, some amplify the psychological depths, and some are in the academic lane.

My lane incorporates all of the above and more as I love to combine its teachings with other paradigms like creativity (visual arts and acting), body and sensory awareness, shamanism, and the Chinese Five Element Theory. Truth is truth no matter what doorway you go through to find it. And the Enneagram is very intimate and personal because it sees us so clearly. That is why I write and teach in what I hope is a user-friendly way. Just as in my private practice, or in my workshops, I play the roles of both teacher and student, so it is my path to share my own stories, struggles, and learnings, and not stand above my reader, client, or workshop participants. I try to not *talk about* the Enneagram types, but rather to *experience* them. I try to own all of them in myself, as they all live in me. As a core number Two I am very relational. I prefer to own my ME and speak directly to your YOU. You are not alone. I am right here with you. I am working on the very same issues that you are. We are one.

I recommend two free online tests that you can take to get started right now: www.eclecticenergies.com and www.Trueself.io. Take these tests as honestly as you can. No one will see the results but you, so there is no need to hide. No one type is better or worse than another. Each number has its gifts and its challenges, its strengths and its vulnerabilities.

Before I introduce the three centers of intelligence and the nine Enneagram roles, I invite you to prepare the receptive field by centering yourself as we did in the Presence chapter.

Actors paint their characters using a vast emotional palette. If they are good actors, they have no preference over "good" emotions and "bad" ones. They feel confident about expressing all of them, when appropriate. Actors who have not done their personal work may be blocked around expressing certain emotions, especially as these particular emotions relate to the bias of their own Enneagram type.

Ask yourself: "What is the emotional palette I paint my life from?"

In the WHERE section we played with our preferential color palette and how we might grow by expanding outside our comfort zone with colors. Now we look at our emotional palette.

As you read through this list of emotions, take note of which ones you feel open towards and which ones you want nothing to do with. Notice your favorite emotions. Notice whether you can allow certain emotions in yourself but not in others. Notice whether they are okay when the emotion is expressed in others but not allowed to be expressed by yourself. Notice whether certain ones are **unacceptable** to you in *any* way.

I suggest you pause after reading each feeling word and check in with yourself honestly. Check in with your body and your heart, and not just your head. You might be surprised about what you are truly open to, and what you are not. Later, you can go back and explore where and when those emotional states got shut down in you. You can also consider how some of these feeling states threaten you so much you want them to go away.

Here we go. Pause as you take in each one:

Angry. Pause. **Jealous.** Pause. **Happy.** Pause. **Proud.** Pause. **Sad.** Pause. **Ambitious.** Pause. **Longing.** Pause. **Passionate.** Pause. **Exhilarated.** Pause. **Powerful.** Pause. **Detached.** Pause. **Rebellious.** Pause. **Driven.** Pause. **Despairing.** Pause. **Provocative.** Pause. **Silly.** Pause. **Sexy.** Pause. **Vulnerable.** Pause. **Afraid.** Pause. **Flattered.** Pause. **Satisfied.** Pause. **Disappointed.** Pause. **Resistant.** Pause. **Content.** Pause. **Ashamed.** Pause. **Protected.** Pause. **Lonely.** Pause. **Overwhelmed.** Pause. **Resilient.** Pause. **Comfortable.** Pause. **Giddy.** Pause. **Superior.** Pause. **Inferior.** Pause. **Empty.** Pause. **Confident.** Pause. **Thwarted.** Pause. **Greedy.** Pause. **Aloof.** Pause. **Devastated.** Pause. **Intimidated.** Pause.

Actors drool over this list. Imagine the late Robin Williams embodying each of them in rapid succession. Magnificent!

And here are three questions that can help you discover more about your relationship with each of these emotional states. Let's use anger as an example.

- *"Am I invigorated by (anger), dismissive of it, or do I feel I must stuff it down because it is bad or scary?"*

- *"Do I accept and embrace (anger) with its many faces, try to understand what it is protecting or revealing, and then try to use it in a productive way?"*

- *"What are some memories I have, pleasant or unpleasant, about (anger)?"*

Your answers to these questions map out your Enneagram type preferences and resistances in the realm of emotions. Let's keep exploring.

The Human-Actor Self Meets the Enneagram

The actor plays a character or role that may be very much like them or quite different. An actor must be able to know themselves well enough that they can bridge any gaps between their way of being and the character's. We human-actors would do well to know ourselves in depth too. Here are a few questions I invite you to answer before you meet the Enneagram types.

How do I perceive myself?

How do I think others perceive me?

Am I accessible?

Do I view others as accessible?

Am I transparent and open?

How do I hide or avoid?

How do I protect myself?

What am I afraid of?

How do I limit myself?

How do I limit or control others?

What moves me?

What holds me back?

At last! Drum roll please!

Introducing... the Three Centers of Intelligence: Head, Heart and Gut/Body

The nine numbers of the Enneagram are divided into Three Centers of Intelligence.

The Body or Gut Center are numbers 8, 9, and 1. Notice they are at the top of the Enneagram diagram. Some of the many gifts of this center of intelligence are its gut-knowing, its high standards, integrity, and its movement towards action, manifestation, being fair and just.

The emotion of **anger** is associated with these styles or energies, and they each express it differently or shut it down. Anger is a resistant reaction to things as they are. Anger has many faces. It can show up as rage, resentment, frustration, as being critical, or disappointed. It can come out aggressively, moving toward the object of its discontent. It can be more passive in its aggression by withdrawing and moving away from that which it will not tolerate. Or it can take a stance of righteousness, expressing that it knows best.

Anger hides vulnerability. Yet when vulnerability is acknowledged it can develop real strength. When we look underneath anger and see what it is protecting, we can move toward forgiveness and true self-empowerment.

There is a counter type in each center, which means that their mask is so well cultivated they may not even sense the associated emotion in themselves, and it may not be obviously visible to others. In this center the **9** is the number who does not blatantly show their emotion of anger.

The Heart Center are numbers 2, 3, and 4. Some of the many gifts of this center of intelligence are an ability to love, empathize, validate others, be of service, achieve goals, and bring forth compassion and understanding.

The emotion of **shame** is associated with these styles or energies, and they each can express it differently. Shame, too, has many faces. Shame grows from feeling bad about how we may have acted, been wrong about something, or not good enough. Shame can show up as blame, victimization, avoidance, humiliation, despair, regret, and over-compensating. It can come out aggressively, trying to deflect its embarrassment and sense of lacking by projecting its shame onto others. It can be more passive in its aggression by withdrawing and running away, giving up or hiding. Or shame can be a martyr, feeling wronged and hurt, so as not to claim its responsibility in a situation.

Shame can catalyze the development of self-acceptance. Through becoming intimate with our shame, we can learn to love others and ourselves unconditionally.

The counter type in the heart center is **3**. Their mask is so well cultivated they may not even sense the associated emotion of shame in themselves, and it may not be obviously visible to others.

The Head Center are numbers 5, 6, and 7. Some of the many gifts of this center of intelligence are its capacity to learn and invent, problem solve, create safety and be comforting, and bring innovation.

The emotion of **fear** is associated with these styles or energies, and they each can express it differently. Fear has many faces too. Fear grows from not feeling you are enough to meet life and its challenges and losses. Fear can show up as a trauma response, which experts in trauma break down into a fight, flight, or freeze reaction.

Notice how you act when you are afraid or feeling threatened or overpowered. Fear can motivate or paralyze. Fear can provoke or tremble. Fear can be controlling and micromanaging, or can collapse into self-doubt and prevent making decisions or setting boundaries.

Fear can be the very thing that develops our courage. In many stories, plays and films it is a fear-based type who becomes the hero, and rises up out of some deep survival instinct and saves the day.

The counter type in the head center is **7**. Their masks are so well cultivated they may not even sense the associated emotion of fear in themselves, and it may not be obviously visible to others.

THE CAST OF ENNEAGRAM CHARACTERS

What roles are familiar to you?
What role most resonates?

We have just discussed fear and the Head types. All Enneagram numbers, however, Head types, Body types and Heart types are driven by a fear of *something*: fear about not having autonomy and control, fear about not having worth and value, fear of fear itself, and not having safety or security.

Before I was even introduced to the Enneagram, as a young acting teacher I saw quite clearly that characters in plays either wanted power/control, validation/love, or security/survival and I taught my students to choose from one of those core motivations when playing a scene or performing a monologue. When I met the Enneagram, it reinforced what I had intuited years before.

I think it is safe to say that most humans know all of these kinds of fears to some degree, but we are each *more* preoccupied around one of these fears in particular. That is how we can differentiate and discover which might be our Enneagram **core** number.

As you look back at the descriptions of the three centers, ask yourself, "Which one of these basic fears is most potent for me?"

In other words, which center speaks loudest to me? Which fear do I default to habitually? As you read more about each individual type ask yourself: "Which of these nine masks, secrets, motivations and strategies do I find myself reverting to frequently and automatically?"

Focus on the motivations especially. Which feel most true to you? Motivations grow from our secrets, which are fear-based. Which of the secrets strike you as most true?

When a person feels truly safe, they can access love and presence rather than their sense of lacking. Characters in a script do not have a point of departure that is coming from love or they would have no motivation to do much at all in the play but just bask in that love. Probably not a play worth seeing.

If we human-actors are feeling completely whole and not lacking anything, then real love is more present and we don't need masks, secrets or strategies. At these times, we can set down our fear-based agenda and then our love based essence moves us. Essence is our purest state of being and it comes from love. It is what most of us want to truly access to feel content in our lives.

Conversely, when we are caught in our Enneagram trance of secrets, those things we hide from others and even ourselves, we cannot come from love; we are motivated by fear and lacking. These motivations are ultimately unproductive in the long run. What we fear is the very thing we end up manifesting.

When beginning a scene, the actor's point of departure is the character's ambition and primal desire. The actor would be wandering through the scene if she didn't understand her character's longing. The character longs for power or empowerment; or she longs for validation; or she longs to feel safe and secure. By the way, safety is not just physical but emotional. When we feel unsafe we feel uncomfortable in a setting or in relation to another person. The actor must distill what her character wants into a simple statement that can grab her in the gut and propel her through the scene. We human-actors have essential longings as well, only we rarely are conscious of these primal desires.

As you are introduced to each number more intimately, listening to their most honest rendition of themselves, check in with yourself and see what brings about a reaction in you that feels like "Bingo! Yes, that's similar to the ME I most identify as."

I introduce the nine core roles as follows: each of the nine numbers has four categories, which are expressed via inner monologue. The four categories are **Masks, Secrets, Motivation**, and **Strategies**.

There are many *look alike* numbers whose **masks,** or facades, have similar features. So you may identify with many masks and even wear different masks for different occasions. Also the **strategies** (the behaviors the numbers use to overcome obstacles that seem to be keeping them from getting what they want) may also seem very close to behaviors you know in yourself. The two things that are most specific and set types apart from each other are their **secrets** and **motivations**.

Secrets are held because we are afraid of something and believe that the revelation of these secrets will put us at risk: risk of being vulnerable, risk of being seen as worthless, or risk of losing our security. As you meet these cast members ask yourself, "Which of these secrets do I keep most often and feel most at risk of sharing?"

Motivations grow from longing for something we don't see that we already have. Longing tends to be insatiable; it is an itch that persists no matter how much you scratch it. If I ask a security type, like a Six, "How much money would be enough to truly feel secure?" they have a hard time coming up with an answer. No amount of money seems to be enough. If I ask a worth type like a Three, "How much adulation would be enough for you to feel like you *are* enough and then stop trying prove your enoughness?" they too are speechless. And if I ask a power type, "How much power and control do you need so that you will never feel vulnerable again?" they refuse to answer such a silly question.

So, which secrets do you keep close to you and which motivation seems spot on?

Finally, our **Strategies** are often not very effective and end up being counter-productive because they are coming from fear and a sense of lacking. In trying to get what we already have (but don't recognize we have), our strategies can ultimately backfire on us and bring about what we are avoiding. For instance, if a Nine (The Peaceful Immovable Boulder) strategizes around avoiding conflict or disharmony, she may enrage the people around her by dismissing or shutting down their resistance, creating a much bigger conflict than if she had embraced the conflict in the first place. This is true for all the numbers. Their strategies can bring about what they are avoiding.

I want to take a moment to remind us that we are not living our lives only from fear and lacking. When we are grounded, centered and in presence, we are able to feel full and confident. At these times we are coming from wholeness; we don't need our masks or strategies. We don't need to hide anything. We can be transparent, honest, shine our light and receive the light of others. Each Enneagram style has glorious strengths and these beautiful attributes radiate through us. The Heart/shame types live through the best part of their hearts, loving and genuinely generous. The Head/fear types live from a sense of having exactly what they need in the moment to meet the moment, and are a model of courage and tenacity. And the Body/power types already feel their **true** strength with no need to hide their vulnerabilities. They can lead themselves and others thinking of the highest good for all concerned.

Number One

Gut/Body Center
Motivation: Power and Control
Associated Emotion: Anger

My Mask
(my public persona)
(what I allow you to see)

I allow you to see my high level of competence and my integrity. I allow you to see that I don't need anyone and that I am strong and independent. I allow you to see that I know what's the right way and the wrong way. I allow you to see that I know the difference between good and bad. I allow you to see a straight, firm and solid appearance. I allow you to see that I mean well when I am controlling the scene we are in. I try not to be angry and explosive, because that is bad, but sometimes things just build up and out it all comes, like a volcano. But I was right all along so it was appropriate to be angry.

My Secret
(private shadows)
(what I don't allow you to see)

I don't allow you to see how disappointed I am in myself. I don't allow you to see that it is really painful to me that people don't hold themselves to as a high standard as I do. I don't allow you to see how resentful I am and how unfair this feels to me. I don't allow you to see how afraid I am to show you how really vulnerable I feel in such a volatile and imperfect world. I don't allow you to see that the reason I am so critical and demanding is that deep down I believe the world will fall apart around me if I don't hold myself and everyone accountable. I don't allow you to see that my inner child believes she is the only adult in the room. I don't allow you to see how much I push my anger down. I don't allow you to see that if I do explode in anger, I become very critical of myself. I don't allow you to see how hard it is for me to apologize and be wrong. I don't allow you to see how overwhelmed I feel by all the demands I place on myself. I don't allow you to see how unsafe I feel and that only the highest levels of perfection can allow me to relax.

My Motivation and Strategies
(basic longing)
(what moves me and how I move you)

Motivation: **I want to be in control.** (autonomy and power at root)

My strategy is to deflect from my powerlessness, helplessness, disappointment and feelings of being overwhelmed by telling everybody what to do and how to do it. I do this in the name of goodness. I deflect from feeling vulnerable by trying to create an ideal world so I will feel safe in it. I take control because I really don't trust anyone else to do it right. I deflect by trying to improve myself and others. I tell myself that I know what's perfect so I can trust myself to make the world right. I work really hard in the things I do, striving for perfection. This gives me the right to control things.

Number Two

Heart Center
Motivation: Worth and Validation
Associated Emotion: Shame

My Mask
(public persona)
(what I allow you to see)

I allow you to see how much I want to be of service to you and the world. I allow you to see my competence and how good I am at providing. I allow you to see that I am a great friend, the person you want to have in your life. I allow you to see how indispensable I am. I allow you to see how self-sacrificing I am. I allow you to see what a good person I am. I allow you to find me attractive. I allow you to see what a generous person I am.

My Secret
(private shadows)
(what I don't allow you to see)

I don't allow you to see how unworthy and worthless I feel. I don't allow you to see that I actually feel somewhat superior to you, that I am a better person than you are. I don't allow you to see that I can feel petty and vindictive. I don't allow you to see how insecure I am. I don't allow you to see that I am selfish. I don't allow you to see that not all my motives are completely altruistic. I don't allow you to see how concerned I am about my image. I don't allow you to see how afraid

I am of your rejection. I don't allow you to see how hurt and resentful I am that I give love more than I feel loved.

My Motivation and Strategies
(basic longing)
(what moves me and how I move you)

Motivation: **I want to feel loved and lovable**. (worth and validation at root)

My strategy is to deflect from feeling unacceptable by focusing on other people's needs rather than my own. My strategy is to know other people better than they know themselves so that they will like me and need me and feel seen by me. I avoid feeling worthless by helping others see their worth. I am self-deprecating so you will tell me I am wrong to put myself down because I really am pretty great. I give good presents. I am sensitive to others, kind and understanding. I try hard to earn appreciation. I am diligent so I can feel like I have left a great legacy and that I am unforgettable.

Number Three

Heart Center
Motivation: Worth and Validation
Associated Emotion: Shame

My Mask
(public persona)
(what I allow you to see)

I allow you to see that I am the best at whatever I put my mind to. I allow you to see that I push through when the going gets tough; I am a work horse and self-starter. I allow you to see that I am a winner, not a loser. I allow you to see how shiny and well put together I am. I allow you to see that I am a hero in my family and at work. I allow you to see that I am worthy of being someone to be proud of. I allow you to see that I am the person you want on your team if you want to win. I allow you to see how much I do (my long *to do* list) and how well I do everything on my list. I allow you to see how noticed and appreciated I am by others, especially important people.

My Secret
(private shadows)
(what I don't allow you to see)

I don't allow you to see my self-doubt or that I feel threatened, which is why I am competitive. I don't allow you to see how exhausted I am and how spent I feel. I don't allow you to see that I get really pissed off if I am diminished in any way. I don't allow you to see how impatient I am and how incompetent I think you are. I don't allow you to see that I really don't think I am enough, or that I ever can be or will be enough. I don't allow you to see that I really don't love myself. I don't allow you to see how self-deceptive and deceiving I can be if I feel ashamed. I don't allow you to see how preoccupied I am with my appearance and how much I care about how you perceive me. I don't allow you to see how hopeless and despondent I can become if I am criticized, fall short, or fail.

My Motivation and Strategies
(basic longing)
(what moves me and how I move you)

Motivation: **I want to be admired.** (worth and validation at root)

My strategy is to deflect from feeling not *good enough* by over-achieving, giving two hundred percent and going until I drop. My strategy is to be very competitive, and to know everything about my competition. My strategy is to out-give, out-hustle and out-perform to avoid feeling *less than*. I go the extra mile so I can feel your adulation. I demand loyalty to feel secure that you will stand by me. I do things to get your attention. I set up a scenario in which I have rivals, and I try to get others on my side because I have been wronged by my competitors.

Number Four

Heart Center
Motivation: Worth and Validation
Associated Emotion: Shame

My Mask
(public persona)
(what I allow you to see)

I allow you to see how interesting and unique I am. Actually, unique is not a strong enough word. I allow you to see that you will never meet anyone like me in the whole wide world. Never, ever. I allow you to see that I am very sensitive and loving. I allow you to see my depth and complexity. I allow you to see how hurt and wounded I can feel. I allow you to see how caring and perceptive I am. I allow you to see my creativity and intensity. I allow you to see how much I bring to the table. I allow you to see how mysterious and unreadable I am.

My Secret
(private shadows)
(what I don't allow you to see)

I don't allow you to see the depths of my despair and hopelessness, only a glimpse of it. I don't allow you to see that sometimes I feel life is pointless, with no meaning. I might share only a glimpse of my depression. I mean, why go on without meaning? I don't allow you to see that my envy is paralyzing. I compare and despair. I don't allow you to see that sometimes I feel mediocre and not at all exceptional. I don't allow you to see all the things that I feel are missing about me and my life. I don't allow you to see how judgmental I am and how insecure I am. I don't allow you to see that I am really angry about how you treat me, revealing only a glimpse of my resentment.

My Motivation and Strategies
(Basic longing)
(what moves me and how I move you)

Motivation: **I want to be exceptional, singular.** (worth and validation at root)

My strategy is to deflect from feeling like I am ordinary by creating a striking image of myself and my environment. I develop myself. I pursue meaning and truth. I make myself pretty elusive. I withdraw and sometimes withhold to make you come find me, so I can prove to myself that I really matter. I avoid the feeling of being mundane or mediocre by disappearing for awhile so I don't have to compare myself. Or I just leave. I set up situations where I do extraordinary things so that I can feel treasured and cherished. When I withhold it signals to you that you could lose me and you must prove to me that I am worth the effort it takes to be in relationship with me. And you will be glad you expended that energy because being with me will elevate your experience of life. I vacillate between inviting undivided attention and disappearing or becoming invisible. I decide between the two opposing states.

Number Five

Head Center
Motivation: Security and Safety
Associated Emotion: Fear

My Mask
(public persona)
(what I allow you to see)

I allow you to see … not much. Or as little as possible. I allow you to see my superiority, and mastery of my chosen interests, though I am also very self-deprecating, especially in a humorous way. I allow you to see that my time and energy are very valuable, and there is just so much of it to go around. I allow you to see that I am a kind person and mean well. I allow you to see my intelligence…when I decide to. I allow you to see that I am observing you. I allow you to see that I am stoic.

My Secret
(private shadows)
(what I don't allow you to see)

I don't allow you to see how afraid I am. I don't allow you to see how deeply I care. I don't allow you to see that I feel a sense of scarcity about many things. I don't allow you to see what I want. I don't allow you to see how unprepared I feel. I don't allow you to see how inept I feel emotionally and relationally. I don't allow you to see how disconnected I feel.

My Motivation and Strategies
(Basic longing)
(what moves me and how I move you)

Motivation: **I want to be abundant, full of resources of all kinds.**
(security and safety at root)

My strategy is to deflect from feeling insufficient by soaking up all kinds of competencies. I retreat while I gather expertise. If I neglect our relationship by not being fully present for you, you will want more of me and I will feel desired. My strategy is to deflect from being transparent by withdrawing and ruminating in a safe place and saying, "Now is not the time." I avoid feeling inadequate and unresourced by keeping my distance and hiding from you. I avoid situations where I may not feel safe and feel threatened. I appear and I disappear. I let you know I need space and that I don't like your intrusion unless you are invited to weigh in by withdrawing and closing off. I am sometimes aloof, which creates curiosity; this compels you to acknowledge my wisdom and insight. I am enigmatic.

Number Six

Head Center
Motivation: Security and Safety
Associated Emotion: Fear

My Mask
(public persona)
(what I allow you to see)

I allow you to see that I am loyal and concerned about our tribe. I allow you to see that I am worried about problems that I see and that I can be helpful in problem-solving them. I allow you to see what a great researcher I am and how I ask all the right questions. I allow you to see that I have a lot of answers. I allow you to see how doubting and provocative I am. I allow you to see that security and safety are very important to me. I allow you to see that I am curious and intelligent. I allow you to see that I can be a good friend.

My Secret
(private shadows)
(what I don't allow you to see)

I don't allow you to see how anxious I am, at least not directly. I don't allow you to see how insecure and uncomfortable I am. I don't allow you to see how superior I feel because of people's incompetence, and how that annoys me. I don't allow you to see how whiny I want to be. I don't allow you to see how stuck and indecisive I am and how hard it is for me to make the right choice. If I choose the wrong thing, I have just made myself less safe. I don't allow you to see how irritated I am about things that make me uncomfortable. I don't allow you to see how intense and passionate I am. I don't allow you to see that I don't trust most peoplr.

My Motivation and Strategies
(Basic longing)
(what moves me and how I move you)

Motivation: **I want to be comfortable and safe.** (security and safety at root)

My strategy is to deflect from my terror by living by the creed "Help me be independent." I use self-defeating strategies of doubting and questioning endlessly so I don't have to make a decision. I am critical, controlling, and micromanaging to make myself feel like things will be done right so I won't be so afraid and uncomfortable. I either go full force into a conflict to deflect around something I am afraid of or I run away and avoid the conflict completely. I avoid anything that can make me feel insecure. I listen to the news, read articles online, and mistrust authority because I want to find ways to feel safe in a dangerous world.

I stay close to people who I know will be supportive of me and not abandon me.

Number Seven

Head Center
Motivation: Security and Safety
Associated Emotion: Fear

My Mask
(public persona)
(what I allow you to see)

I allow you to see how much I can do. I never stop doing. I allow you to see how I can juggle lots of things at once. I allow you to see that I am a happy, cheery person with a positive outlook on life. I reframe anything negative into the bright side. I allow you to see how I approach my life as an adventure, and so I am interesting and fun to be around. I allow you to see how enthusiastic I am. I allow you to see how I have endless energy. I allow you to see that I am the kind of person who rarely says no to anything. Because I do so much, I learn so much and can advise you about a lot of different things, and I like to do that. I allow you to see that I have a great imagination and lots of ideas.

My Secret
(private shadows)
(what I don't allow you to see)

I don't allow you to see how much anxiety I have, and maybe I don't allow myself to see it either. I don't allow you to see how much I worry. I don't allow you to see that I can be judgmental. I don't allow you to see how overwhelmed I can get about choosing just one thing, when I want so many things. I don't allow you to see that I am insecure. I don't allow you to see that I am scattered. I don't allow you to see how much I avoid my feelings (unless they are positive) and how I really want to avoid your uncomfortable feelings as well. I don't allow you to see how ill at ease I get around your pain or my pain and want to distract from it quickly.

My Motivation and Strategies
(Basic longing)
(what moves me and how I move you)

Motivation: **I want to be limitless.** (security and safety at root)

My strategy is to deflect from anything negative by shutting it down or denying it. I distract myself into the next shiny project. My strategy is to be so busy that I don't have time to dwell in the pain of life. I steer away from conflict and deflect around people's anger and discontent. I try to be upbeat and distract everyone else into happiness. I avoid feeling unhappy by reframing on the spot. In order to feel like I am getting the most out of life, I draw on an unlimited supply of energy. Since all I want is to be healthy, happy, and live forever I run away from my fears. I say I don't want to live in fear, but actually I am afraid of being afraid.

Number Eight

Gut/Body Center
Motivation: Power and Control
Associated Emotion: Anger

My Mask
(public persona)
(what I allow you to see)

I allow you to see how strong I am and how I can easily take charge. I allow you to see that I am high-status, that I really am the Alpha in the room. I allow you to see me as a protector for the greater good. I allow you to see how just and fair I am. I allow you to see how helpful I am and how capable. I allow you to see my commanding presence. I allow you to see that I can be reassuring and with me in the scene there is no need to panic. I allow you to see my anger and disappointment in things as well as my passion and gusto. I allow you to see how I get things done and expect others to do the same.

My Secret
(private shadows)
(what I don't allow you to see)

I don't allow you to see how vulnerable and misunderstood I feel. I don't allow you to see that I actually feel inferior to you. I hide that. I don't allow you to see that I wish someone would watch my back just as I watch theirs. I don't allow you to see that I need reassurance too.

I don't allow you to see how burdened I feel by all my responsibilities. I don't allow you to see that I know my power is an illusion. I don't allow you to see that my anger is really fear and resistance to the way things are. I don't allow you to see that deep down I feel powerless and out of control. I don't allow you to see that the demands on me are too much for me.

My Motivation and Strategies
(Basic longing)
(what moves me and how I move you)

Motivation: **I want to be powerful.** (autonomy and control at root)

My strategy is to deflect from feeling vulnerable at all costs. My strategy is to take charge and keep moving. My strategy is to demand that people follow my lead. My strategy is to push myself hard. My strategy is to threaten to leave if I don't get my way. My strategy is to withhold approval and affection if you don't meet my standards or if you try to challenge me. My strategy is to let you know I don't need anyone. My strategy is to avoid feeling any fear by making you afraid.

Number Nine

Gut/Body Center
Motivation: Power and Control
Associated Emotion: Anger

My Mask
(public persona)
(what I allow you to see)

I allow you to see what a kind and easy going person I am. I allow you to see how I put your needs over mine and rarely say what I want. I allow you to see how evolved I am as a person. I allow you to see that I am above pettiness. I allow you to see that I am content and that nothing much bothers me. I allow you to see that I am perceptive. I allow you to see that I am watching you but not revealing much of me. I allow you to see that I am not high maintenance. I allow you to see that I believe that conflict is unnecessary.

My Secret
(private shadows)
(what I don't allow you to see)

I don't allow you to see how I really want respect from you. I don't allow you to see when I am angry and resentful. I don't allow you to see that I would like some attention too and do want to be seen and valued. I don't allow you to see how I feel like I am always sacrificing. I don't allow you to see how really powerful I am in my quiet way. I don't allow you to see that I am really not as calm as I appear. I don't allow you to see that I play with words and don't tell the whole truth in order to feel powerful. I don't allow you to see how afraid I feel when there is confrontation.

My Motivation and Strategies
(Basic longing)
(what moves me and how I move you)

Motivation: **I want to be important and matter.** (autonomy and control at root)

My strategy is to deflect from feeling vulnerable by acting as if things don't bother me. My strategy is to shut down any conflict in the name of peace and harmony so I can look superior and more evolved than others. My strategy is to move in and out of visibility and use that as a way to gain power in a situation. My strategy is to smile when I am angry and not let you see how I really feel. My strategy is to skirt a disagreement by agreeing. My strategy is to avoid showing you I am in pain by saying, "I'm fine." My strategy is to be immovable unless I choose to move.

✸✸✸

How change happens within each type

For self-realization and true transformation to occur we must have the courage to set our masks aside. We can set aside our masks by consciously choosing to do so, or because we are forced to. The Wizard of Oz had no choice about this, because his curtain was pulled back and he was exposed. In that moment he had to adjust and be honest about who he was. Oz became human, and out of his humanity he could illuminate the truth for Dorothy, the Scarecrow, the Tin Man, and the Cowardly Lion. He gave them the essential message that they already had within themselves that which they thought they lacked; their secrets and fears had been lies they were telling themselves. Oz had this realization about himself, too. He had been fooled by the idea that power came from an external display, rather than the simple reality that he was already a wise and powerful person.

We can certainly change our secrets by deciding to reveal them, first to ourselves, then to others. In revealing our secrets and especially challenging their veracity, we can discover they are lies, and we can be freed from them and be empowered by the unveiling of them.

We have the power to change what we think we want (our motivations and intentions) as well. We can say "Do I really want power or can I gift myself with the notion that I am already empowered?" "Do I really need adulation to prove I have worth or can I offer myself acknowledgment and appreciation?" "Do I really need to be comfortable or do I already have within myself what it is I need to meet this life and create comfort?"

The strategies I use to get what I want change when *what* I want (my motivation) changes. My motivation changes when my secrets are exposed. The need to wear a mask changes when my fears and sense of lacking dissolve. Then my essence emerges and charisma and presence replace the mask.

How do I set down my mask? I set down my mask with courage; I must have the courage to acknowledge that I am wearing one. How do I reveal my secrets? I must have the courage to know that I have secrets and to look at them. How do I shift my motivation? My motivation can change simply by taking a pause and saying to myself, "Are the things I fear real? Am I really lacking these things or do I actually already have them within me?" My strategies change when they follow my new motivation.

The character in a play operates from the trance of his secrets; he believes his secrets/lies are true and his motivation is created from them. But we as human-actors are not trapped by these scripts. We can write ourselves beyond them.

WHAT'S UNDERNEATH?

ACTORS ARE DETECTIVES. They interpret the evidence from the text to make seen and heard what the playwright or screenwriter has left to the imagination. They get clues from the text to find the subtext, and they ask the right questions to get to what's hidden. Subtext is the truth that lurks underneath the lines. Subtext exists in poetry, too. Sometimes an enigmatic poem needs decoding to unpuzzle its trickery, just as an actor must do with a script. This chapter is about how we, human-actors, can access our secrets and how to find out what is underneath the masks we wear.

As human beings we, too, have subtexts. We don't always say what we mean. Sometimes we do this on purpose to consciously hide our truth. Remember each of the Enneagram personae (masks) has their secrets. Each of us buries our secrets with the belief that doing so will keep us safe. Sometimes we push our truths down so far beneath the surface that we can't even find them ourselves, like a set of lost keys. The result is that we can only speak honestly to the degree that we are aware of what lies beneath.

This is self-deception. We deceive ourselves and don't even know we are doing it. That's why I believe that using only a talk therapy modality, as opposed to experiential or body-centered therapy, is limiting because the client can only speak to what they are conscious of. A good therapist digs around by questioning and challenging her client in order to excavate the depths of the unconscious, attempting to reveal the unseen subtext. Human-actors also need to be detectives if they are to live with greater awareness.

In the chapters on Charisma and Presence, we discovered that the body never lies. When we observe the body carefully, learning its language, we find buried memories and truths that go unnoticed if we only listen to ourselves talk. That is why my therapeutic work is body-centered. Every cell of the body has a mind, and the body is not inclined to hide what's on its body-mind.

We can only speak the truth to the degree that we know it, and that means getting to know what is unconscious, which can surface through our body, if we pay attention to it. That's why when people take Enneagram tests they may not always come up with their accurate core type, because they have answered from text (their knowing on the surface) instead of from subtext (their secrets).

When I trained to be a body-centered psychotherapist, it was easy for me. From my acting experiences I resonated with the concepts of presence, body language, intentionality, back-stories and how each narrative from the Past informs each and every action and reaction in the Now.

One powerful way I can help a client reveal to themselves what's underneath (subtext, secrets) is by using a body-centered method called Gestalt therapy, a therapy that was developed by the late Fritz Perls. Gestalt therapy is marvelously theatrical as it utilizes dialogue, body sensing, and the context of scene. It uses these acting techniques to resolve past and current wounds and conflicts. These unhealed places are projected onto new players, as the client unconsciously tries to play out and work through these painful, remembered but buried scenes from the past or hiding in the unconscious mind.

Therefore, the person we are struggling with in the present has others standing behind them from the past; our reactions to painful situations in the present are amplified by old scene partners from the past. We are rarely aware of this, because that which hides in the shadows also hides from *us*.

One way to shine light onto our shadows is to use what Gestalt therapy calls *empty chair work*. As an example, I ask a client to sit in a chair and speak to an empty chair facing her, and to imagine she is talking to a person she has an issue with. She gets to say everything she may be afraid of saying directly to that person. She can let it all hang out, unedited. It is, after all, only a rehearsal. This gives the client a safe way to find her voice. So next she is asked to sit in the empty chair and feel what it is like to *be* the other person. She has to committedly enter the other person's world. She becomes the other person and has to give that person a voice too. In this way the client experiences the missing link, which is that her point of view is not the only point of view. The conflict or misunderstanding begins to lose energy and may ultimately dissolve.

In this moment, empathy is found. On some level the client can understand and actually experience the other's feelings and behaviors, and hopefully she will recognize that those very same feelings and behaviors exist in herself. I have her bounce back and forth between the two chairs until the dialogue has found its resolution, and greater understanding and empathy have been achieved.

I have created art for the chairs that I use to do chair work. One is the **I Feel** chair. This chair has a person depicted with their mouth open. Swirling energy moves from the person's heart outward from their mouth. On the other chair I painted a person looking at her reflection in a pool of water. There are also small mirrors decorating the back of this chair. This is the **I am You and You are Me** chair.

I use chair work like this on myself when I am stuck in my own Enneagram fixations, ruminating over a feeling of being disrespected, or a sense that I had been treated unfairly. Quite simply, I do this activity when I have lost my way. I find it opens me up to so many more options, a new way of seeing this particular scene in my life, and I find greater empathy for the other person and for myself too. It is hard being human. We need all the help we can get.

And the most incredible thing about this activity is that on some spiritual dimension, the rehearsal actually turns out to have completed the scene. Clients will come back the following week and I will ask them if they had that practiced conversation with their co-worker. They frequently respond: "I didn't need to. They were completely different to me and I to them. Everything had already shifted."

Now how does something like that happen? Jung's view of collective consciousness offers one theory: their consciousnesses are linked on another dimension. Or perhaps the shift has occurred merely from touching into empathy; the "I know that in myself" part creates a bridge where there had been only disconnection. Or maybe the dialogue actually happens on an energetic level just by doing the work, openly and committedly, during our session. It has freed up the protected places, taken down the walls. The egos have spoken as have the higher selves.

It is especially powerful to have my clients, these very human-actors, talk to a deceased person with whom they had not made peace or said all the things they needed to say, before the person died. There is a great opportunity here to reach a completion, to transmute anger or disappointment, to find or ask for forgiveness, to offer or receive gratitude. Of course, it is all pretending, just as the actor pretends. And it is just as real as anything in this life of ours is real.

Empty chair work can be used in a myriad of ways. With actors I use this to bring forth their director-observer self and to help the actor stop judging their character. A dialogue is created between the actor-self and the director-self. Being the director-self empowers the actor to see things about his performance he had missed. By embodying another point of view both actor and human-actor see things in a new way.

In this work it is as important to observe body language as it is to listen to what is being said to the empty chair. In life, we would do well to pay much better attention to what our bodies are revealing, so we can live more honestly and consciously.

Another way I use Gestalt techniques with actors is to invite a conversation between actor and character. I ask the actor to sit in one chair, and to imagine that the character she is playing is sitting in the empty chair across from her. I ask her to talk to the character and tell the character what she (the actor) appreciates about this character. Then I have the actor sit in the character's chair and become the character talking to the actor in what has now become the empty chair. I ask the character to tell the actor why that actor is the *perfect* person to bring the character to life: what qualities they share and how they are aligned. I invite the character to tell the actor a secret about the character-self that is buried inside the script. Identifying the character's Enneagram type also gives us insight into those secrets.

Finally, I have the actor return to her own chair and finish the dialogue. I invite the actor to tell the character why it is perfect that they have come together at this time in the actor's life, and the many blessings and gifts she knows she will receive from playing the character.

The actor and the character become friends. The actor can no longer judge the character because they have formed a bond.

Even if the character is a villain, the actor can find that potential within her own unclaimed shadow parts. Claiming our shadows makes us more whole. Playing villains can be very therapeutic for an actor. Embodying a person we are in conflict with, as human-actors, provides us with similar benefits. It becomes a bridge.

I will tell you that when I auditioned I did this exercise with myself and the character I wanted to be cast as. Even if I did not get the job, which was sometimes devastating, I would still feel grateful that I had made a new friend, and received what I needed to get from the role I was auditioning for. I didn't really need to play the character to receive the benefits from getting to know her.

Enneagram secrets are clearly exposed in empty chair dialogues. Our Enneagram style and accompanying misguided beliefs are driving most of our conflicts. The Enneagram in conjunction with chair work makes a wonderful team. Try it yourself and see.

I also use this very same empty chair work with clients to focus on hidden tensions *inside* of themselves, their own *inner* cast of characters. We each have an inner cast, made up of the different roles we have played in our lives and our Enneagram access points.

For example, what happens if my inner Two (Giver) wants to deflect away from her own needs, let's say her writing, and my Three (Achiever) wing is pissed off that the Two won't push forward and complete the next book? "Just do it!" exclaims my Three. Then my Four (Unicorn) chimes in saying the concept for the book isn't special enough, it's already been done and she agrees with the Two that it's best just to focus on helping others accomplish things. In despair, my Four withdraws her much needed energy from the creative process. My Eight (CEO) then asserts that the Three is right and taking action is the best course for all concerned, but my One (Improver) declares that the whole idea of the book is far from perfect and that I should wait until I have improved on the thesis. What's the point in expending the energy if it won't be perfect?

At these times I set up chairs and enact a play with myself, letting all parts vent and be heard. And, oh yes, all the parts vigorously argue among themselves. Let me tell you this is very exhausting. But it is even more enervating to let these wars between my parts continue their battle unseen, unheard, underground.

Freud pointed out that often the things that drain us most are not happening outside of us, to us, but rather within us. I do a workshop called The War Within that reveals our inner resistances and how we can mediate these conflicted, undermining parts.

Finally, I summon my director/observer/teacher/peacemaker self and have her walk around all the empty chairs of my inner cast, and see from outside of the scene how to satisfy all of their needs, how to create a cooperative, co-creative inner ensemble. I guess the experiment worked, because you're reading the end result!

The word gestalt literally means the *whole* that is more than the sum of its parts. In Gestalt therapy we become aware of the concept of foreground and background. In film acting terms: what are we looking at in a close-up and what are we aware of far away in a long-shot? The long-shot creates the background. For the audience it is subliminal, yet provides the context for the scene. Imagine ways in your life, as a human-actor, where you are only looking close up at a scene you are playing out with your boss, or partner, or friend. Everything your boss is doing now seems like the whole picture, amplified and true. At this point you are only aware of the foreground.

That's why we say things like "You *always* do this!" "Always" becomes the operative word because the camera of your mind only lets you see or feel the close-up. Gestalt therapy invites the background (long-shot) to trade places with the foreground (close-up) and from this new focus so many new things can be seen. What's underneath floats up to the top.

Presence is so important it has its own chapter in this book, as it needs to be accessed by the human-actor to live a more complete life. Presence is a big part of Gestalt therapy. We find presence through the body. What are you aware of in your body right now? Are your feet planted firmly on the ground? Do you feel the support of the chair or the floor? And then what arises through your body after centering? What is in balance and what is at odds? What is open and what is closed?

An actor must become like a clean white canvas in order to adapt to and reveal the balances and imbalances of the character he is playing. He does this by finding presence first. From this place of neutrality, the layers of the character can be disclosed to the audience.

As human-actors it serves us well if we ground ourselves and find presence before playing out our scenes at home or at work. Remember the pause. From this place of presence or neutrality receptivity is enhanced. The body feels strong so the heart can be open, and the mind unlocks from its rigid thinking into a place of understanding and connectivity.

Another vital element of Gestalt therapy is its focus on personal responsibility as opposed to victimhood. I ask myself, "What am I responsible for, what is truly mine to hold?" I don't need to hold more than what is mine. I stop using words like, "That person made me feel this or that." I take that power away from them, and kindly acknowledge my feelings as my own. And I have discovered those feelings through unmasking them. The other person didn't *make me* feel anything; my own feelings surfaced because I was triggered by my Enneagram secrets being exposed, and experiences from my past that exaggerated and reinforced that trigger.

That's why it's so important as human-actors to understand our Enneagram triggers. If I am a gut type, it is likely that the other person I am playing a real-life scene with has uncovered my feeling of vulnerability and powerlessness. If I am a heart type, the trigger will probably be that I feel judged, demeaned, or belittled, revealing my sense of not-enoughness. If I am a head type, my trigger will unmask that I am afraid and not resourced or competent enough.

As human-actors we must disclose our secrets to ourselves. Understanding our Enneagram tendencies helps us with this. Then when we are ready, and have sat with our feelings as long as we need to, we can begin to change our relationship to the triggers. We can do this privately, or with a neutral witness or therapist. We can fully and honestly express ourselves from our emotional palette, and see these triggers with fresh eyes. We can bring closure to unfinished business because it is **our** business to finish. We reframe past experiences, seeing them as lessons that made us wiser and stronger, and ultimately free ourselves to move on and flourish. When we are ready (and only then) we can set down the role of Victim, recast ourselves as Survivor, play that role for a while, and finally recast ourselves, yet again, as Thriver.

Freud said, "Unexpressed emotions will never die. They are buried alive and will come forth later in uglier ways."

One can see how valuable this process of working with our triggers can be for us to use in our real lives. We can revisit a less than successful scene we played out with a check-out person at the grocery store, or with a friend. By stepping outside of the role we are playing with the other person we can access our blind spots, and even consider a better way to play out a similar scene in the future. Through this kind of work we access the UNDERNEATH, the unconscious, the subtext, the truest of truths.

Bottom line, it is natural to wear masks and have secrets with the intent of keeping ourselves safe. But there are dangers to wearing masks unnecessarily. We sometimes perceive threat when it is not there. In these moments we aren't looking at the situation clearly, that there may be no threat at all, so we just habitually wear our masks, thinking we need them. In time the mask we wear can become indistinguishable from our very own skin. And from that place, we cannot play the scenes of our lives with intention, presence and pure potential.

"We all understand how dangerous a mask can be. We all become what we pretend to be."—**Patrick Rothfuss, American writer**

OUR SCENE PARTNERS

I DIRECTED A YEAR-LONG acting group called "The Company" when I was in graduate school at Northwestern. I was a graduate assistant and my job was to teach acting and text analysis, create a cohesive ensemble with the actors, and adapt scripts that we would perform at school and also take on the road. Imagine this short little redhead, sitting on pillows driving this huge bus out of town with The Company. Trust me, I would never be cast in the role of the bus driver.

This cast of students was quite extraordinary, and a few moved on to become formidable actors and directors. I'm not going to name drop here, but they were and are an impressive group.

When I was in the role of student my teacher, Frank Galati, would conduct a really cool choral activity. We would form a circle with him standing in the middle and he would recite a phrase from a Vladimir Nabokov novel, or a line of poetry. We would repeat back what he said, trying to stay in sync as one voice. It was a brilliant exercise. Maybe at first some voices stood out but we would keep repeating and repeating until we became one voice. Then Frank would change the script. He would chant, "Now we are one." We would repeat "Now we are one." He'd say it again and we would follow again and again until our voices were, in fact, ONE.

I didn't realize then that this was a spiritual task.

I stole Frank's marvelous experiment and took it into every acting class I taught and every show I directed from then on. It not only humbled each of us, but created a sense of safety, and a powerful team. The Company rehearsals always began this way, only now I was the one in the center deciding the lines that would be repeated. I expanded and enhanced it to make it our own, but we always ended with the chant, "Now we are ONE. ONE. We are ONE. We have won! ONE."

We met a few times a week so we did this regularly and the glue between us stuck. There were no stars. We were ONE.

One day my father came to a rehearsal and witnessed something miraculous. I was playing with the concept of us being one body as well as one voice. I turned off the lights and we could barely see each other. I invited the company to get on the floor, somehow stay completely connected to one another and move as one entity. By this time, we had even learned to breathe together, one inhale and one exhale at a time. While they were negotiating the floor, breath by breath, move by move, I began our chant "Now we are ONE." They repeated in one voice. "Now we are ONE." They repeated. "We are ONE." They repeated. "We have won. ONE." Again, they repeated. I invited these phrases periodically as they moved and each time, immediately, they chanted back in perfect harmony.

Then, I really don't know why I did this, but I chanted, "I am ONE." Pause. No answer. My father's eyes widened. Mine widened back at him. I chanted, "I am ONE." Still no answer. And I chanted again, "I am ONE."

Silence, as they continued to move as one body. My father gasped, then covered his mouth. There was no I. Ego had dissolved. There was only a WE. And the WE was ONE.

The image at the beginning of this chapter shows the ensemble of Enneagram types with the diagram at the center. The Enneagram symbol and drawing is a whole circle, an **O**. What if we could play the scenes of our life remembering "We are ONE" with an **O** at our center instead of a mask?

One of the things that unnerves me around how some teachers convey the Enneagram is that it becomes a way to distinguish us from each other, and to separate us. And I believe that is one reason why some people choose not to learn about it. It can create divisiveness and that is a breeding ground for judgment, prejudice and stereotyping. That is why I call my Enneagram teachings, *Nine Paths to Oneness*.

9 Paths to Oneness

Our world does not need more paradigms to espouse non-inclusiveness. As I explained in the chapter My Role-Who am I?, at its best the Enneagram gives us an understanding of who we think we are, with all the gifts and limitations that come when we type-cast *ourselves*. The knowledge the Enneagram provides is invaluable in identifying our motivations and patterns, so just maybe we can dis-identify with them. We then can open up to the possibility of embracing all our Enneagram lenses.

That is the goal. We do have a core number and many other access points that become our defaults when we are living unconsciously. But I cannot stress enough, all the numbers live within us, either clearly visible or relegated to the shadows. We **are** ONE.

Let's say a playwright creates a character. That character is limited by the parameters of her story. The character cannot grow beyond the script that has created her. It is the actor's task to bring that character to life while staying true to the text.

The actor, however, has his feet in two realms. He must play the character with only as much awareness as the writer has allowed. The actor might be more evolved personally and spiritually than the character he is playing. Still, he must let his character live in the character's world, from the perspective of the character's Enneagram type. The actor must let the character travel the journey that has been laid out by the text. On the other hand, the healthy actor, hopefully, recognizes the ensemble and his service to the whole, like the WE-ness and Oneness shared by The Company.

In real life the human-actor has the possibility to be conscious and to rise up beyond his ego. The human-actor, if he so chooses, has only pure potential in front of him. He need not be limited in his perceptions and reactions unless he is very much attached to them. He is not stunted by a text that confines him. In a later chapter we will see how each of us can rewrite our script if we have a different desired outcome.

Why bother with all of this? Why rewrite our scripts? Why not just accept the ME that we think we are and stop right there? We bother because when we move through our play or Hero's Journey intentionally and with awareness, very simply, we avoid our own suffering and create less suffering for others, our scene partners. We bother because our soul seed has come here to grow and blossom.

Growing ourselves does not mean that we don't accept the ME we appear to be. We must try to accept all that arises. I once heard Eckhart Tolle, author of *The Power of Now*, say in a lecture I attended years ago: "We are not that which arises, we are the field it all arises from."

In the field of our being there are glorious flowers and there are weeds and invasive plants. I can pull out my unwanted weeds because it is my garden and I choose to. Inevitably, those weeds will return. And I can pull them out again or let them grow free without my tending, though then they will strangle out the more delicate plants I intentionally planted.

So, as I try to ascend the spiral of my Hero's Journey I feel it is my duty, as the caretaker of my soul seed, to continue to pull out the weeds of my misguided thoughts and beliefs, my overreactive emotional states (honoring them but not fueling them), and my insensitive, non-empathic and unkind behaviors.

Life is fragile. We can be here one day and gone the next. Tomorrow we might not get to resolve our poorly played scenes and may not have the chance to be kinder and more compassionate. We may not be able to make amends for our misdeeds. I have witnessed this with troubled couples where one person dies suddenly. I have watched others end their marriage in divorce and then move on to choose someone just like the partner they left. This happened because they had not grown more aware or changed anything in themselves from the first failed relationship. We can choose to play the scenes of our life unconsciously, reactively, and with habitual patterns that only stop in a dead end. Or we can remember the soul seed that is here to grow and learn and become much more than who it thinks it is.

If we begin with the premise that all the Enneagram numbers live in each of us and we try to get to know each type better, not to divide us but to bring us closer together, then we are living from a place of emotional intelligence and true empathy. Imagine how this change in perception could improve our relationships and our lives.

When a scene with our scene partners in life is going poorly, it's time to pause and observe. As soon as we realize, "Ah, I know that in myself" the other person stops being the enemy. We can recognize at least part of the issue as a projection out of us, and it is more likely that a meeting of the minds and hearts can take place. It is not our goal to remove responsibility from our scene partner for what they have done. It is our goal to own all our own responsibility and learn not to be victims or perpetrators.

Usually in plays and films the characters do not have this capacity to empathize and resolve their conflicts so kindly. In fact, that is the very thing that makes the stories interesting and exciting to us. The characters are not more evolved than we are, and so they are relatable. Hopefully we can even learn something from their mistakes. Profound writing and performance give us this. The characters grow before our very eyes and we grow with them.

By knowing all the Enneagram styles well from the inside out—their masks, secrets, motivations and strategies—we can develop rapport and fellowship with each other, if we choose. We can know our scene partner's vulnerabilities as our own vulnerabilities, his shame as our shame, or her fears as our fears. We can understand why he feels the way he does and perceive the situation the way he may perceive it. We can build a bridge over the chasm between us. The soul of the Enneagram does not want us to use it to manipulate others. I believe it was given to us to bring us closer together; we can recognize that We are ONE.

WHAT DO YOU REALLY, REALLY WANT?

WHAT IS THE difference between what ultimately is our life's purpose and what the ego believes will make us happy? The ego operates from insatiable desire-driven ambitions. These have little to do with what our higher self or superconscious was truly sent to do or be. What we really want is to find our true vocation, and once found to live it in the most authentic way possible. When we are moving down our true path we don't need masks, secrets and lies.

Most of us want to feel safe enough to remove our masks, set aside the need to keep secrets, and to move more creatively through our lives. But the misguided beliefs stemming from our Enneagram types keep us from seeing things clearly. We have to challenge the lies we tell ourselves. Most of us, deep down, want to learn how to love and feel loved for who we are.

On the other hand, ambition is connected with our ego's zeal. The ego needs to aspire actively, set glorious goals, and create a target which is often unattainable. If it is attained, another ambition quickly replaces the first. Our short-term story of goals met may seem like a victory, but in the long run life will teach us that those were superficial and ultimately unsatisfying.

In the most important theatrical stories ambition never wins the day. Perhaps goals are happily achieved but as they are reached, something backfires and creates misery, until hopefully the hero claims what they are truly meant to do or be, even if they had never seen it clearly before. Shakespeare's Macbeth and his wife are devoured by ambition. This insatiable ambition creates havoc and pain for themselves and the people around them.

In David Whyte's magnificent book of essays called *Consolations* he addresses this beautifully. *"Ambition is a word that lacks any real ambition, ambition is frozen desire, the current of a vocational life immobilized and over-concretized to set, unforgiving goals."*

What is our personal vocation that is immobilized by ambition? Vocation is our life's purpose, our calling in the grander scheme of things. David Whyte continues:

> *... a true vocation calls us out beyond ourselves; breaks our heart in the process and then humbles, simplifies and enlightens us about the hidden, core nature of the work that enticed us in the first place. We find that all along, we had what we needed from the beginning and that in the end we have returned to its essence, an essence we could not understand until we had undertaken the journey.*

Another illustration of this concept can be found in the Wizard of Oz: there's no place like home. Only when each character or human-actor has taken that journey down the yellow brick road, faced their inner and outer witches (or dragons) and conquered their fears about what they feel is lacking in themself, do they realize their true vocations.

When I was a little girl my mother told me I was meant to be a teacher. I was in second grade and did not like that proclamation. It felt limiting to me at the time. In those days girls were teachers or nurses or stay at home moms, and weren't encouraged to consider being anything other than those roles.

There was nothing wrong with those roles, in fact, they were completely honorable and important. It just didn't feel like she was really seeing me. My brother, however, was told he ought to be a doctor. My mother had longed to be a doctor herself, but had been discouraged by her father, who was very much a misogynist. My grandfather had killed her dreams and disconnected her from her perceived vocation. My brother was invited to fulfill those dreams. I was not.

It so happened that at that time, when I was seven, I had the very best teacher of my whole public school life. Her name was Barbara Kohl, and I loved her. I felt *she saw* me. She made a profound imprint on my soul. I was an excellent speller and Mrs. Kohl told me that during spelling time I was to walk down the hall to a first-grade class that Mrs. Taylor taught, and tutor the "younger kids." I took this very seriously and created lesson plans and games to play with the first-graders to help the challenged spellers learn to spell in a fun way. I felt needed and important, and I was a very good teacher.

I was also a very good little actor. My father and I would perform scenes from plays and musicals for organizations, women's clubs, etc. He was very hard on me and expected a lot, and I became hard on myself as well. The experience of acting was filled with both pleasure and pain. I liked pretending to be someone else, enjoyed feeling empathy and understanding the character's psyche while releasing myself from some of my own darkness. I did not like disappointing or displeasing my dad or the audience so I pressed myself to be perfect.

This acting thing seemed like a far more interesting path for me to take than being a teacher. So, I followed it.

Still this teacher-self never seemed to fade from view. I had to illuminate. I couldn't help myself. Learning seemed so very important to me. After my freshman year of college I taught in a summer program at Northwestern. I continued to act and loved it, but what was acting if there was no psycho-spiritual dimension to it? It had to mean more. Acting had to be part of something bigger.

As it turned out, my mother had been right all along and had indeed seen my true vocation. She saw my purpose before I did. My ambitious ego self had other ideas. My ego thought that the actor's path would be a more powerful way to prove my worth, something I felt was lacking. My ego was not considering that there might be a way to incorporate all my gifts. I must add that my mother was always supportive of me. She came to every show I was in and was never discouraging of anything I did. She just saw what I could not see. Of course, I would incorporate all my skill sets into the process of teaching, learning and growing. That was a given to her.

As David Whyte points out, on our way toward recognizing our destined vocation our hearts will feel broken. We will be misled and humbled by ambition, before we land precisely in the core nature of our true work in this lifetime.

Over the years, I've consulted with an author, teacher, counselor and Shamanic practitioner named Jose Stevens, and each time I work with him I feel blessed. A light goes on. Among other modalities, he works with a channeled personality system called *Personessence*. This is based on the Michael teachings that proposes that there is a "group soul, a collective consciousness of 1050 essences." It is a fascinating paradigm that comes from the premise that we have many lifetimes, that our soul hopefully matures with each lifetime, and that through all these lifetimes we have a core role.

It is a complex system that I encourage you to explore. If you go to www.thepowerpath.com you can download a free e-book that Jose has written and generously given away. The seven roles in the *Personessence* model are: artisan, sage, servant, priest, warrior, king, and scholar. These roles incarnate with learning curves that may span through as many as one hundred lifetimes or more. Young souls may appear as infant kings and still be presidents of countries, immature as they may be.

Jose can immediately identify your role. I thought he would say that I was an artisan. In fact, my role is sage. This coincides with my true purpose as a teacher. It turns out that many performers and artists come in to a lifetime as the role of sage. Robin Williams was a sage. My father was a sage. A political leader can be a sage as well as the Dalai Lama.

No roles are better or worse than any other role, much like the Enneagram. There is no hierarchy in these paradigms. A servant is just as important as a priest, a warrior as important as a king, just as every character in the play is part of the whole and an equally necessary cast member. Each role has a growth trajectory, and a hero's journey to travel. And like the concept we have explored about the ascending spiral each role in the Personessence model can circle and evolve through many hero's journeys and through many lifetimes. Each lifetime offers the pure potential of maturation and enlightenment.

Hopefully, in this world of ours, there are enough older, more mature souls to balance out the foolish and harmful ambitions of the younger ones. Jose is one of the many spiritual teachers who see life as a play where we are given the same role through many lifetimes, and where our intention is to master and attain the true essence of that role.

From my point of view, the Enneagram shows us clearly the roles we have chosen to play, the thoughts and feelings associated with those roles, and the motivations, strategies, behaviors, and secrets of those roles. And so I never stop referring to it. It is my companion.

In some New Age teachings there is an idea that we are the captains of our own destiny, and that concerns me. As I discussed in the first chapter of this book, I believe there is a both/and operating at the same time. We must act *as if* we have choice and free will because that is our story to write and rewrite. **And** we must accept that there is something bigger than our little self which moves us toward a destiny. These paradoxical viewpoints actually work hand in hand.

In some New Age teachings people are encouraged to make daily affirmations. There is no harm in this if it helps us get in touch with living a more intentional life. The question I must ask is; **who** is doing the affirming? Is it the ego, the small ME, teamed with ambition, trying to prove something from a sense of lacking, who is creating these affirmations? Or are these affirmations a conversation with the Universe, inviting a creative collaboration on behalf of the highest good for all concerned?

In my role as a life coach, I am most interested in the last of those three questions. What is your purpose for being here, how are you meant to grow, and what is it you have to offer mankind and the planet? We explore purpose over ambition.

In my role as an acting coach, I am attending to both tracks: the egoic ambition driven track as well as the essence-driven track. In the first track, as an acting coach I am trying to help the actors construct believable characters who are ambitious. We know that plays are rarely written about the enlightened ones. So, our focus is on the character's ego structure which is what drives them through the play.

We have examined that what drives a character in a play comes from a feeling of lack, a hunger. As David Whyte points out, "*...we had what we needed from the beginning...*" though the character never knows this. Only the enlightened soul knows this. We must identify the character's ambition in order to enact their story accurately. Their human ambition is what drives the scenes, not their ascended or transcendental selves.

Also in the role of acting coach, I attend to the second track, that of the personal development of the actor, for his own Hero's Journey. I am inviting the actor himself to connect with a greater purpose. When he does, the creative force, Consciousness, moves through him and inspires his work and his own life. I encourage the actor to look for something in himself quite different from ambition. I ask the actor to focus on things he can *give* rather than what he hopes to *get*. This empowers the actor and nurtures a feeling of success, in a professional arena full of rejection and perceived failure. I believe an actor's ability to endure his chosen art form is directly related to his focusing on *giving freely*, rather than *achieving fame and fortune with avarice*. In this way, he "comes to" his art form from a sense of fullness instead of scarcity.

When actors go to an audition, what do they want? Is it just to get the job, or is it more than that? Landing the part is something they have little control over. There are so many factors that are being considered by so many people. The actor will, more often than not, come out of the experience disappointed and feeling he has failed.

If an actor focuses on getting cast at his audition he is setting himself up for failure, except for the lucky one who is chosen. However, if the actor goes into an audition with a different kind of intention and attention, like bringing joy to himself, being fully present, connecting with new people or old friends, playing and having fun (after all it is called a play), plugging into something bigger than ambition (to be successful, rich and famous), then the audition itself becomes the gift he gives himself. He is much more likely to leave the audition behind him as a pleasant memory and move on, having already fulfilled one task of his vocation.

We can see how the same principle can apply to going to a job interview in any profession or going on a first date. I ask the actor before an audition: "What is the gift you want to give yourself?" I begin each and every class or workshop I give, on any topic, with the very same question, "What has brought you here and what gift can you offer to yourself?"

Notice I am not interested in what they want from me or from the class itself. Their energy is directed toward an absolutely attainable gift, because there is not anything external stopping them from bestowing that gift upon themselves. There are only inner obstacles to deal with.

So, let me ask you: "What has brought you here and what gift can you offer to yourself?" Maybe you have decided you want to conjure up the courage to do something that's out of your comfort zone. Maybe you want to stay connected to your body, your presence, and not be influenced by other people's projections onto you. Maybe you want to be open to discover something about yourself that you have never seen before. Your intention or desire is received by you as a gift you can give yourself.

Sometimes when I would be on my way to teach an evening acting class, exhausted after a full day of working: acting, teaching, writing, or directing, and being a mom, wife, and daughter to boot—I would ask myself before entering the theatre, "Ruthie, what gift do you want to give yourself tonight?" Often the answer would be, "I want the class to teach itself."

The very best classes and inspired teachings grew out of this invitation to myself.

One time, during a monologue class, I asked myself to not work so hard or force anything brilliant to come from myself, but rather to just get out of the way. I discovered something wonderful which I have used over and over since in many aspects of my teaching, around all kinds of subjects, in many arenas. After an actor performed her monologue, I asked her to come out into the audience and immediately play a new role. I asked her to pretend that she was a great director/ teacher who had just witnessed the monologue. I left a chair on the stage (so this is similar to chair work) to represent the part of herself who had just performed. I told her that she really liked and respected the actor and that her intention now was to direct the invisible actor and give her helpful and inspiring feedback that was descriptive, not evaluative.

In this way, the actor-self had to engage her observer-self, and be able to give new and insightful information to the part of her that had just performed. It was uncanny. It seemed every actor who tried this was able to see what needed to be seen, to say exactly what I, as their teacher, might have told them.

The best part of this was that I got to rest, witness, observe and learn! It was a win-win for the actor who had performed, for the other actors who were observing the process, and for me.

When I was a young acting teacher, actor and director, I read the book *Conversations with God* by Neale Donald Walsch. In that book he breaks human motivation down into two categories: fear and love. This intrigued me. I pondered, "What drives us?" The answer would apply to any character we might be playing.

What I came to see, long before I was introduced to the Enneagram map, is that most of us rarely play the scenes of our life from love, though we may think we do. Most of us always have an "agenda", conscious or not. Our ego has an ambition that it feels will satisfy a need to feel powerful and in control, to feel validated and loved, or to feel safe and secure. Most of us want something we think we don't have and believe if we get it, we will be happy...until the next thought of lacking arises.

In the Hero's Journey the hero comes from a place of lacking; otherwise why would she be on a quest in the first place? There is fear driving this feeling of lacking. The following list of fears all connect to numbers on the Enneagram, starting with number Seven:

- a fear of missing out (#7)
- a fear of not being in control (#8)
- a fear of not being important (#9)
- a fear of not being perfect (#1)
- a fear of not being lovable (#2)
- a fear of not being enough (#3)
- a fear of not being special and valued (#4)

- a fear of not being resourced and abundant\ (#5)
- a fear of not being safe (#6)

The characters in a play must always come from this hungry place. This longing is what drives them, though they may not confess it. Instead they usually keep their longings secret and masked. We human-actors do the same thing around our fears or sense of lacking. We become ambitious and this covers up the deeper mission. Ambition is like putting a band-aid over a primal wound.

In David Whyte's essay on "Longing" from *Consolations* he reminds us of what aches underneath ambition. "... *Longing is divine discontent, the unendurable present finding a physical doorway to awe and discovery that frightens and emboldens, humiliates and beckons...*"

In the previous chapter on Entrances and Exits I invite us all to pause at a doorway (a literal one or a metaphorical one) before entering. This is when we have an opportunity to get in touch with our longing. It is our longing that is connected to our Hero's quest, and that formulates the intention of our journey.

Wanting something we think we don't have is vulnerable. Very few of us reveal directly what it is we really want. We dance around it or call it by another name. Many of us become disconnected from the source of our longing.

When we long for something we are hoping it will fill up our empty places. These holes inside of us are born with our egoic structure and are not experienced by us as beautiful or valuable; they feel shameful, like something we must keep secret. At the same time, we love our longings, are attached to them, and consider them an essential part of our identity. Our Enneagram numbers all long for something they feel they must hide to keep safe. Once again the concept of opposites is at play here; we are attached to our narrative and our longings *and* we are ashamed of these unfulfilled or *less than* places.

David Whyte adds: "... *Longing has its own secret, future destination, and its own seasonal emergence from within, a ripening from the core, a seed growing in our own bodies...*"

Remember our soul seed, dropped onto this earth to learn and grow in this lifetime. Perhaps the greatest lesson the soul seed is meant to learn is that what it longs for, it already has within itself.

The Enneagram types possess both ambition and longing. Their ambitions are what create the masks they wear to cover up the vulnerable longings they feel. Characters in plays engage their audience with the honesty and boldness of their longings. We human-actors have the opportunity with empowered intention and embodied presence to realize that we already have within us that which we believe we are longing for. It came with our soul seed, fully equipped, and pointing toward our purest potential, that of restoring our wholeness. Remember in the Wizard of Oz, Dorothy always had the power to return to home.

In an earlier chapter we explored the various roles Enneagram types play: their masks, secrets, motivations and strategies. Their motivation is what each type *thinks* they want. But here is what I believe each of the Enneagram types *really, really* wants:

#1
One really wants to remember that she is already perfect in her humanness. She wants to lay her burdens down.

#2
Two wants to remember that he is acceptable and worthy of love.

#3
Three wants to remember that she has nothing to prove and that she is enough.

#4

Four wants to remember that he has no missing pieces and that his inner light shines through like a harvest moon in the night sky.

#5

Five wants to remember that she has all she needs within her to meet the world and that she has plenty more of herself to share with others.

#6

Six wants to remember that he is safe, at home with himself, and that there is always support within him and around him.

#7-

Seven wants to remember that she has all she needs to feel whole, secure and complete.

#8

Eight wants to remember that he need not hide his tenderness from others and that he can trust enough to follow as well as lead.

#9

Nine wants to remember that she is important, has a right to be seen and heard, and that the peace she seeks never leaves her because it comes from within her.

WHAT'S IN THE WAY?

WHAT STANDS IN the way of getting what we really want?

We are in the way. Our perceptions are in the way. Our attachment to who we think we are is in the way. Our fear of being more expansive and whole is in the way.

In the Hero's Journey the character determines what they want (their quest), and then goes about trying to attain it. In any good story, and in life, the hero will face some obstacles.

If we all got what we truly wanted right away what would be the point of telling our story? Imagine this story: So and So was born, got what they wanted, continued to get what they wanted, got more and more of what they wanted, lived their whole life getting what they wanted, and then they died peacefully in their sleep. Boring!

The obstacles we face are both outside of us and within us.

What makes life not boring is that we are presented with many challenges. These are the external dragons we must strategically tame. But the internal challenges are the most limiting because they hide and control us.

Michelle Cassou is a master teacher of process painting and author of the wonderful book *Point Zero: Creativity Without Limits.* Just as I use the overlying metaphor of the theatrical kingdom as illuminator to show us how we can live our lives more consciously, Michelle Cassou uses the medium of creativity and painting to do the same. She speaks of three dragons that block the energy flow of inspiration, intuition, and living in pure potential. These dragons have all been revealed in our Enneagram secrets and motivations. See if you recognize any of them in your kingdom.

- the dragon of judgment/product (an outcome-driven dragon)
- the dragon of control (a fear-driven dragon)
- the dragon of meaning (an idealizing and imagination-driven dragon)

As soon as one of these dragons appears for an actor their artistic expression shuts down. This was a handout I gave actors in my classes:

For actors, judgment (the first dragon) will strangle an opportunity. Dare to ask these questions and then try to answer them in your acting work.

- *How would you act if you could cross the lines of acceptance and the predictable?*
- *How would you act if there weren't any consequences?*
- *How would you act if you could exaggerate?*

- *How would you act if you could do nothing at all?*

- *How would you act if you could be really bad?*

- *How would you act if you could let the work surprise you?*

- *How would you act if you could be silly and childlike? If you were only three years old and it was okay to let that child out to play with you right there with her?*

- *How would you act if you didn't know how, if you didn't know the right way, if you didn't know anything?*

Michelle Cassou says, "The mind acts reasonably. Intuition is wild and unpredictable."

- *How can you let intuition lead the dance with your mind?*

- *How would you act if you could go slow, then slower and slower?*

- *How would you act if you could go faster and faster?*

- *How would you act if you could allow yourself to be really ugly?*

Let's substitute the word live for the word act and see what happens to predictability in your life:

- *How would you Live if you could cross the lines of acceptance and the predictable?*

- *How would you Live if there weren't any consequences?*

- *How would you Live if you could exaggerate?*

- *How would you Live If you could do nothing at all?*

- *How would you Live if you could be really bad?*

- *How would you Live if you could let Life surprise you? If you could be silly and childlike? If you were only three years old and it was okay to let that child out to play with you right there with her?*

- *How would you Live if you didn't know how, if you didn't know the right way, if you didn't know anything?*

- *How would you live if you could let intuition lead the dance and let your mind follow?*

- *How would you Live if you could go slow, then slower and slower?*

- *How would you Live if you could go faster and faster?*

- *How would you Live if you could allow yourself to be really ugly?*

See what happens to the Dragon of Judgment if you allow these suggestions. Is he tamed? How might intuition join you on your journey? Might synchronicity and good fortune appear more often? Might pure potential lead you in your Becoming?

The primary obstacles within us are the false and limiting beliefs about who we *think we are* and what we think we are capable of experiencing in our lives. The Enneagram shows us our false beliefs. The Enneagram doesn't tell us who we are; it reveals to us who we *believe* we are. The Enneagram map of our self-deceiving patterns guides us, first by giving us the keys to unlock the prison door that confines us, and then by showing us the path to claiming our soul seed's hidden treasure.

As an audience member watching a play or film, we can perceive flaws in the character's self-perceptions. We want to speak out, "No! Don't you see? You are wrong about what you are thinking about yourself and the situation! You are going to get the opposite of what you want. You are bringing to yourself the very things you fear!"

Yet we continue to play out the same blind spots in our own lives.

Another inner obstacle is resistance. This can be like all three dragons rolled into one. Resistance is very hard to overcome because it acts insidiously and covertly. Bringing our resistance into the light and honoring it at first, getting to know why it believes it is helping us, is the beginning of transforming it. As human actors we think we want to change, but do we really? Are we not more comfortable in the status quo, playing our roles as we have always played them, like a very, very long run of a play?

How do we collapse the status quo gently to allow for pure potential?

I must bring Jose Stevens, my counselor and shamanic guide, into this scene of the book as well. He shared a magnificent ritual with me that I want to share with you.

First, stand with your eyes closed and imagine where in your body the status quo (your stuck place) lives. Is it your gut, your heart, or your head? It can be anywhere. Then you imagine something moving out in front of you from that point; it could be a laser beam of light, or a zig zagging line, whatever your intuition shows you. Imagine this channel moving out from this point into infinity. There is no end. Then you start asking "What if" questions to the Universe. You engage in collaboration, not trying to control how things will unfold.

We can use the Enneagram to help us ask some of these questions.

One—What if I could trust that everything was unfolding perfectly just as it is?

Two—What if I could truly know I didn't have to earn my right to live?

Three—What if I could stop forcing things to happen in order to prove I was enough?

Four—What if I could claim my magnificence and never feel that it is threatened?

Five—What if I could feel the abundance rather than scarcity and share myself freely?

Six—What if I could feel supported in every moment without doubt?

Seven—What if I could enjoy the stillness and the pause and feel its fullness?

Eight—What if I could live without hiding my hurts and tenderness under a display of anger?

Nine—What if I could feel the importance of sharing myself and my wisdom without withholding or controlling?

After you have thrown those "what if" questions into the channel of infinite possibilities, you imagine there is a sparkling crystal stone dropping down through the crown of your head and collapsing the vertical stagnancy of the status quo. The crystal lands in the place of your primal wounds and, like a stone splashing into the infinite ocean of pure potential, it sends your "what if" questions in all directions, 360 degrees around you. Your message has been heard by collective consciousness; you have removed What's in the Way, the status quo collapses and co-creation begins.

THE REWRITE

W HAT IF YOU could imagine that your life is a dream? What
if you could imagine that just as you can wake yourself
up from a dream you are having at night, you can wake
yourself up from the dream you are living in your life's dream-play?

Let's say you can't erase what challenges have confronted you in
your dream or in life, but you can rewrite your perceptions around
those challenges. You can re-perceive them. And you can rewrite how
you play the scenes because of those new perceptions. And you can
come through those challenges, victorious.

Sometimes, when I am having a disturbing dream, I command
myself to wake up. I sit up in bed and say, "I don't like how this dream
is going. How do I want it to go?"

Then, in my sleepy cloud of thought some message comes to me; it gives me a way to rewrite the movie I am dreaming so it doesn't disturb me so much.

I go back to sleep and the movie-dream begins again, but this time I willfully include edits and changes; I am the writer of this dream-movie, after all. Sometimes my unconscious mind takes hold again and veers me back to those disturbing images or scenes, but I get to wake myself up again, ask for inspiration, imagine some rewrites, and perhaps even recast some of the characters. This happens very quickly as I am really wanting to go back to sleep. "I need to sleep!" I say to myself, "So let's start the rewrite."

I close my eyes once again and dream into something that feels more in alignment with where I want this dream to go. Of course, I am never completely in charge. There is a collaboration between my conscious mind that wants better outcomes; my unconscious mind that is holding unresolved issues and old patterns and speaks to me in dreamy metaphors; and my superconscious mind which is limitless and infinite and has a higher perspective than the other two minds. The superconscious would only give me this dream in the first place if it knew I was ready to receive important information from this dream-movie.

When I had bad dreams as a little girl, I would shuffle in the dark to my parents' room. I knew I needed to wake my mother up for help. I would stand next to her and whisper, "Mommy, I just had a very bad dream."

My mother, deep in her own dream, would say, "That's nice, dear." And she would return to her own dream-movie. I would stand there and wonder, *Does she mean that, or is she just still asleep?*

This was quite an interesting moment for my little girl self. "That's nice, dear." Maybe it *was* "nice." Why not? Even though I was very scared and still quite upset from the bad dream, perhaps she was right. I could consider it.

But then I realized that she was out of her mind. How could any of that nightmare be "nice?" *What was she thinking?* King Kong just paid me a visit again and was smashing our neighbors' houses under his gigantic feet. His enormous eye was looking in my bedroom window. I wanted to say to my mom, "Wake up, lady. A monster is at our front door!" Instead I said, a little more loudly, "I'm scared to go back to sleep because I might dream it again."

Then she would say, with her eyes still closed, half in her world, half in mine, "Go back to your bed. You choose what to dream. Dream about dancing in the Nutcracker or something wonderful."

I paused. *Okay. That could be fun.* By then I had calmed down. I walked more decisively back to my room (although I paused at the door to make sure King Kong's eye wasn't still looking in).

I climbed into my bed and did what I was told. After all, I was a good girl. Yes, I might have enjoyed a little cuddle in their bed, or having my mom walk me back to my room and hold me until I fell asleep. But in some amazing way, because she did it her way, I built a resourcefulness for myself around my dream-life. I became the master of my own dreams. I was in charge of them. I became empowered around my dreams. They were my stories, after all.

I believe that gave me a new way of viewing my waking dreams as well. How do I dream my day? What costume will I wear tomorrow? What's the storyline going to be?

As I have worked with my dreams over the years I have developed a narrative voice that speaks aloud to me while I dream, like a voiceover in a film. Perhaps that voice is connected to my superconscious mind. It will say, "Oh, this is happening in this dream because you need to look at this or that." Or it will say, "Your impending death isn't real; it's just making you face an ending of something. What is that something that is ending and beginning?"

It is a very wise and reassuring narrator; it has insight and a healthy point of view. I believe we can all develop that voice, whether we are asleep at night or awake in the day. It's all the same.

I have not always lived my life from this truth, this knowing that I can wake up from my suffering. There are times I forget that I can wake up from the dream-play, and instead toss and turn throughout my day in rumination and despair. Sometimes I feel held captive by the life-dream. But eventually I realize that if I let myself forget to wake up, then that is also a dream I have written. I must even *like* this script a little. It might even be "nice."

There are nights when I am very brave. I may choose to let an unsettling dream unfold in its own way, because I feel it has come to bring me some uncomfortable message or reveal a blind spot. My mother encouraged me to change the story line completely, moving from King Kong to dancing in a ballet. But that would mean I would dismiss why King Kong showed up in the first place. Maybe I needed to experience this nightmare for a reason.

At these times I choose not to wake myself up and rewrite or edit. I choose to go through the unpleasant ordeal, like watching a thriller or horror movie, and then unpack the metaphors in the morning. Why do that? I suppose a part of me feels the need to learn something from that particular dream-movie and doesn't want to mess with the script.

Sometimes I am in the mood for a tearjerker, and will choose to go to a very sad movie so I can cry and move the sad feelings that are already inside of me. Maybe I just need to have a pity party for the character in the movie and myself simultaneously. No harm in that. It's quite therapeutic. Or I might want to see an action film because that mirrors something in me that needs to be aggressive. Or I may need to go to a silly, inane comedy because I have been holding my life too tightly and need to lighten up and be childlike and goofy. It's all available to me. I can watch a movie at the theatre or I can dream-live the same movie, by day or by night.

In life, we find ourselves struggling with the same issues, revisiting our work around our vulnerabilities, shame, and fears. We may notice that we have recurring dreams at night, too. We may feel like we are circling the same drain. Remember my belief that life is like moving in a spiral, simultaneously repeating and ascending. My unnerving dream about King Kong coming to our neighborhood and destroying the homes around me is an example. But King Kong never destroyed our home. He repeatedly peered his one enormous eye into my bedroom and then put his finger through my window. Somehow, though I was still terrified, I knew he didn't really want to harm me. He was as interested in me as I was in him. After all, I had cast him in my dream. There was something lovable about this big beast, even to my five-year-old self. In time that dream became less scary. I knew he was coming to teach me something about safety and my own ability to tame what in my life might appear as monstrous. I kept rewriting the end of this dream movie until ole King Kong became my friend. And then I never dreamt that dream again. I didn't need to.

My ongoing relationship with dreams helped me realize that I could play the scenes of my life, no matter how disconcerting, with intention, strategic decision making, and finally I could transform my demons into friends.

As I continue to apply this to my personal growth, I have found that I can eventually dream and then execute the changes in my life that I believe I long for. I can budge the stuck places, the reruns of my life, when I am ready to do so. I have found this takes dedication, time and patience. It took many rewrites of my dream about King Kong until I could metamorphose his threat to me into a refuge. I continue to rewrite my limiting narratives and I suppose I always will. We do what we do until we don't do it any longer.

I ask myself, "Who is the Dreamer of this dream, the player of this play? Who wants this dream-play to be different? Who longs for the change that I believe I seek? Is this Who bigger than my egoic structure, my Enneagram energies? Is it more akin to my essence and my part in the collective One? Am I ready to join the collective One, as the individual ego in The Company dissipated and joined the collective We?"

Is all of me ready for this change, for new ways of playing the scenes of my life, for continuing my process of becoming more than who I think I am? Is the whole cast of characters within me, all my Enneagram access points, on board to be a unified ensemble moving together toward my sense of wholeness and the successful completion of my Hero's Journey?

As we contemplated in other chapters, different parts of ourselves have differing ideas about what's good for us, about whether we should change the script. If we do, how would we rewrite our dream-play?

Some parts of us want to cling to the story they know, and those parts are very powerful in holding us to our old script. Like a bad Hollywood sequel with no fresh ideas, these other parts of us are afraid to rewrite the dream-play, and in their powerful resistance they will keep the story going the way they know it goes.

These parts need to be seen by our narrative voice (our director-witness, observer-audience), unveiled, and then befriended. Remember the Wizard of Oz? When the great Oz turns out to be just a sweet little old man, wise and dear, with self-doubt and good intentions, it took little Toto the pup with no ego to sniff him out and pull back the curtain. When Oz was seen as he truly was, small, beautiful and human, his vulnerable, best and whole self moved into visibility, and he helped Dorothy and her gang while he helped himself. He changed. He went home to Omaha in his hot air balloon with a *new vision* of himself. He could have returned to Omaha before, but he wasn't ready to rewrite his dream-play until he encountered some new cast members, Dorothy and her tribe.

Before we can rewrite our dream-script, we must know all the characters well. We must see the saboteurs, expose them kindly with understanding, and get them on board for the rewrite. We must unite them and befriend them, as I did with King Kong, until we don't need to keep dreaming that same old dream, or playing that same old play.

And we must continue to strengthen that all-seeing narrative voice that knows all aspects of our dream production well, and also knows how much it is ready to evolve.

DROPPING THE MASK

A T THE END of a play, a curtain call usually takes place. The
fourth wall, that imaginary space between the audience and
the players, is broken. It is no longer invisible. Though the
performers may still be wearing their costumes, the masks of the
characters they played are taken off. They are supposed to bow or
curtsy as themselves, not as their characters, or at least present some
version of themselves. The audience applauds and acknowledges that as
witnesses they have been there all along, watching, even participating

in the theatrical experience. In film or TV, the screen displays a running list of credits, and therefore there is a disconnect between actor and audience. In a stage performance, actor and audience must finally meet face to face and recognize their relationship. This is another part of the magic and intimacy of live theatre. Perhaps it is also why we see more and more films including bloopers and/or outtakes during or after the closing credits. A smart marketing move by film execs; not only do the credits get seen, but the actors and process also can be shared with the audience. The audience leaves feeling included and part of the process, instead of just being witnesses. The disconnect is diminished.

Now, how do we come out from behind the curtain in our own lives? When will we stop hiding? And who is our audience?

The answer will be different for each of us. Some of us may be afraid of abandonment if the people who mean the most to us see the things we are hiding behind our curtain. Others of us may believe God is watching and the responsibility and expectation to live by a moral code is what makes us afraid of being seen completely. For still others, perhaps they are their own audience, with their own high hopes, and so they live in self-deception so as not to disappoint themselves.

I hated the curtain call when I was a young actor because I was stuck on wanting some anonymity. I wanted to remain as just the character in the audience's minds forever, and then I wouldn't have to come out from behind my very own personal curtain. I was shy and guarded. Maybe some people didn't experience me that way, but it's true. It felt much safer to hide behind the character I was playing. And honestly, I felt exposed to their possible rejection of me. What if the applause was lukewarm? What if they threw tomatoes?

I didn't realize then that the audience was entitled to be seen and heard as well. They were entitled to have their opinions, judgments, projections and resonances. I hadn't yet learned how to make this revelation of my Self safe for me.

As I have discussed in both my books, I am a core number Two on the Enneagram model. Many Twos prefer to be the wind beneath others' wings, prefer deflecting attention to the *other* to avoid being revealed or judged themselves. They protect their fragile sense of their own worth. And at the same time, we Twos do want to be seen, as long as it is in a positive light.

All Enneagram numbers play with visibility and invisibility, but with different motivations.

For a Nine, it might be to give them a sense of power. After all, disappearing from view, hiding your true feelings can be a very powerful tactic. Camouflage can win many a battle.

For a Five, playing with being seen or not seen may have something to do with feeling secure or not. "I will only come out when I am ready, prepared, and feeling fully resourced to meet this moment."

For a Four, moving out of sight, while staying energetically present invites their scene partner to come find them. This proves their desirability and value. Some Enneagram teachers refer to the Nine, Five, and Four as the withdrawing or withholding styles. And it makes perfect sense why they do what they do when they feel as they feel.

The truth is that when I was on stage or even on-camera I loved standing under a beautiful rose-colored spotlight, as if the Source itself was shining that loving light on me. I drew energy from that light, and presence, and I emanated charisma. There is another metaphor here: **When we embrace the light, we are all capable of shining it right back as well.** This is true on stage or off.

I was sneaky and deceptive, though. I was using the character to protect my sensitive ego, while savoring the fact that my ME was very much there as well, standing right with my character, basking with her. Remember the secret of the Two is that they don't deeply feel their innate worth and that on some level they are unacceptable. Twos live their lives trying to prove otherwise. The character I was playing gave me a kind of armor against experiencing the displeasure of others. And yet, the most important person I was fooling in this ploy was myself.

"No man for any considerable period can wear one face to himself, and another to the multitude, without finally getting bewildered as to which may be the true."
—Nathaniel Hawthorne, The Scarlet Letter, 1850.

When I was a young college student my teacher, Frank Galati, said that sometimes we can be most ourselves when wearing a mask. I went on to explore this as a teacher myself, giving many mask workshops and inviting the actors I worked with to allow the mask to slip at strategic times during a performance, so that the audience could get a glimpse that there was indeed much more behind that mask.

On the back cover of this book I reveal many of the roles I have played on and off stage. I have played daughter, wife, mother, auntie, friend, teacher, and therapist, plus all the paid roles I was cast in. After creating this collage of photos, I realized that I could identify all nine numbers of the Enneagram as roles I have played. What are the roles you play? Can you identify them? Can you own them or do they own you? There is nothing wrong with donning these masks. What matters is that we are conscious of the fact that we are wearing them. And when vulnerability is called for in precious relationships, when speaking the truth from our essence is essential for intimacy and love, we must have the courage to remove the mask and set it aside.

Very early on as a child actor, when I shared my aversion to the bow with my mother, a wise and experienced audience member, she told me I was being selfish. She insisted that I learn to be gracious rather than deprive the audience of their expression, whatever they thought, whatever their experience. She said that it was like rejecting *them*, rejecting a gift they wanted to give *me*. She told me that it was my responsibility to receive generously. She said I had to practice this. The truth is that through all my curtain calls, throughout my acting career, the audiences were always generous, and I had to continue to learn to be generous with them as well.

As I take this same exploration into my personal life, I remember how hard it used to be for me to receive personal compliments. I know many who have this same difficulty, who seem genuinely embarrassed by praise. I could always celebrate others unabashedly and truly mean it, see the beauty in others and proclaim it. It is easy to appreciate the good in others. It is organic and natural. I have worked hard to learn to receive validation personally, just as I learned to do it onstage.

Some teachers of the Enneagram say that Twos use compliments as a way to seduce or manipulate. This has not been my experience, and over the years I have had many Two clients. If anything, I believe it is an aspect of our shadow self, giving to others what is not easy for us to give to ourselves. This principle is true for all the Enneagram styles, each in their own way, each with their own issues; what is effortless to give may be hard to receive.

An Eight might find it difficult to allow others to protect them when they are very much at ease with protecting those around them. A One may find it hard to receive feedback for improvement, yet it may be much less of a struggle for them to give advice to others, stating their view of the right way or wrong way. A Six may be able to point out the problems inherent in an idea and suggest (out of her own anxiousness and desire to control her fears) ways to do it better and with less risk. Yet that same Six might not welcome others trying to control them and tell them what they should do.

Each of the Enneagram energies has the task, if they are to earn their bow at Curtain Call, to work with their discomforts and non-habitual patterns.

The psycho-spiritual practice for Twos is to stand in our rose-colored light without apologies or shame. That is why the word humility is associated with the Twos. Humility means the honest assessment of Self. Humility does not mean self-deprecation. It means being able to be as generous to ourselves as we can be to others. In a sense, it means that on the stage of life, we must authentically, expansively, and conscientiously act out our roles, and be our own generous observer/audience as well, applauding our own triumphs, and appreciating, with gratitude, that we are honored to be an aspect of the great expressive Oneness.

Just as my mother suggested long ago that I learn to receive applause graciously, I have negotiated this receptivity, personally, when someone shares how they value me; I try to let it in. I try to feel into it, not pridefully, but generously. I also realize that the person offering praise could not do so if they did not recognize those same qualities in themselves that they are admiring in me. I always try to mirror this back to them after I have received their offering fully into my heart. The heart feels full and as if it has lived its purpose. I say, "Thank you, and you know you couldn't say this to me if that very same beauty didn't live within *you* too."

This kind of mirroring transcends pretense and allows equanimity and intimacy. The grand spotlight of Presence shines on both of us simultaneously. And I believe this is as it must be. The scene of recognition is best played mutually, as we are reflections of each other and the Divine.

I have a confession. I have a cabinet where I keep thank you letters from clients, students, relatives, and friends. I always say I will organize them someday. Then I tell myself that when I truly have come to love, accept, and appreciate myself unconditionally, I will let them go. I have not reached that destination.

I am embarrassed to say that sometimes I think one day, when I am gone from this life, my son will read these letters, and see me through other people's eyes. He has often said he has a life-time subscription to The Ruthie Show. This stung me the first few times he said it. But now I understand that he is a cast member of that show, and an audience member to boot.

I am coming to embrace my son's terminology and the truth of it. When I am feeling hard on myself, I return to that cabinet and randomly choose a few notes to read. I weep because those people could see me, receive something from me, and experience the impact I had made on them, when I so easily forget and become blind to what it is that I bring. In the cabinet I found a book of poetry I had written when I was about eleven or twelve. The poetry was filled with despair, revelations of the dark places I hid from others, and the never ending need to prove myself. That little one still lives in me. I hold her and rock her as I know well her longing in myself, even now, to be enough, to be worthy of the gift of this life.

CURTAIN CALL

Ruthie playing Colette in college

I MENTIONED IN THE chapter called Hero's Journey that people often ask me if I miss acting. I am well aware that the skills I developed, even the talents I was born with, have never left me. I practice everything I learned as an actor, teacher, adaptor, and director each and every day of my life, personally and professionally.

To return to this question about whether I miss being on stage,

I will be completely honest, as I have tried to be throughout this book. I will begin by saying that even though there are many things that I do *not* miss, I am deeply grateful for those things now, and for the many lessons I learned from them. They prepared me for life in so many ways, even though they didn't feel comfortable to me at the time. And the whole theatrical package led me, without doubt, to this and all the other Acts of my life-play. I wouldn't have skipped those experiences for the world.

This is what I do not miss: I do not miss the politics and networking that the actor's life so demands. Those of you who think the actor's life is exciting and alluring, think again. It's hard on so many levels. I do think the ME that I am now would be more effective at handling those challenges than I was able to do back then. The irony is that as an author, facilitator of workshops, and therapist/coach in private practice, I continue to have to embrace the marketing world in order to continue to get more work. So, one cannot run away from these resistances. They will follow you wherever you go, whatever you do.

I do not miss the hurry up, wait, wait, wait, hurry up. An actor has to be ready at a moment's call for an audition or for their turn on the set. They are just a small part of a bigger picture that includes all aspects of the whole production. Even the leads, the famous ones, experience this. Yet viewing this from a higher perspective, all of our lives (whether we are actors or not) are about *hurry up...opportunity is here right now and we have to show up and grab it. Wait, wait, wait...patience, sometimes the timing of doing something is not yet right. So, what might I be doing, preparing, or learning in this waiting period? Hurry up...seize this moment, no resistance, the time is NOW, to align with what I have been waiting for all along.* Once again, the actor's plight and the ways of the human unite. I can run but I can't hide from my discomfort.

I do not miss the constant rejections, looking for the next job to support my family, though in this area too, I have grown to realize and accept that I can't be everything for everybody and that being chosen is so subjective. Maybe I have a braver heart now. I don't know. I do know I am not the right friend for everyone. I understand I am not the right teacher for everyone. I am fully aware that everyone won't resonate with how I do or see things.

I do not miss being called "talent" instead of by my name, treated like a commodity or a product, though it is completely understandable why this is how it is in the biz, with so much money at stake, and so many players in the production. I really do not fault anyone in this. It did cause great discomfort to my ego, but everyone was doing the best they could, playing their own roles, struggling with their own dignity and self-respect and going after what they wanted.

I do not miss the scarcity and competitiveness and lack of generosity of spirit that can be a part of the actor's community. But guess what, my current chosen profession, my vocation, displays that very same feeling of scarcity, with a sense that there is not enough work to go around. The psycho-spiritual work is to remember that there actually *is* enough to go around, and to counter the opposing viewpoint of *not enough* with abundance thinking and cooperation. What is the highest good for All, remembering that I am a part of that All?

I do not miss the traps of fame, and watching actors suffer as they dream of their big break that may never come. As the Tao Te Ching asks of us, "*Fame or one's self, which matters to one most?*"

I remember my mom always saying to my dad, "You just wait. You are going to get a series, I know." She said this to him even after he had turned 80 and was still a working actor, albeit not a famous one. He never did get his series, but he was an artisanal sage, and financially supported himself and his wife in his chosen art form. And this is nothing different for people in all lines of work: the entrepreneur dreaming of fame and fortune, the salesman like Willy Loman in *Death of a Salesman* by Arthur Miller, waiting to make it *Big*.

Here's what I *do* miss: I do miss the incredible process of examining text and, like a good detective, solving the code of a character I am meant to play. I do miss all that is discovered about myself when I work to bring a character to life. I do miss the rare moments of intimacy and incredible nakedness when playing a scene with a fellow actor and being able to meet them and know them *heart to heart*. Yet I notice that all of these things are incorporated in my current work as a therapist, coach, author and workshop facilitator.

I miss working with my *techies* who would present me with a costume or a wig that became the missing piece to unlocking a character. And the lighting designers who created god-like ambience with colors, patterns and light. And the set designers and sound designers who gave my character a home, a context, a world. I guess I continue to play with this in working with my husband to create our beautiful garden and welcoming home.

It's a cosmic joke. The things that I *do not* miss have followed me and are present in my life every day. And the things I *do* miss are manifested and reward me in my true vocation.

There is only one character I want to reconnect with and dream to embody anew. I hope to be able to give myself this gift someday. Perhaps. Her name is Colette.

When I was in college, my mentor, Dr. Robert Breen, adapted a three act play for me of Colette, the magnificent French writer, actor, and philosopher. He somehow knew that this was a character I had to play, befriend, and merge with. He was so right.

Bob Breen shaped how I learned, how I *came to* a text, and how I viewed the world. He taught me the difference between descriptive as opposed to evaluative criticism. This was my first introduction to the neutral compassionate observer self. I guess he was my Zen master. He taught me how to create safety for myself and all the people I would be working with: actors, artists, musicians or clients who are on a path to self-realization, living more consciously, and lessening their own suffering. Shortly before he died, at our last meeting, we spoke about what direction my life appeared to be moving in. I suppose he knew it was headed in this direction all along. And that must have been why he had introduced me to my beloved Colette. By intersecting her Hero's Journey with mine, he set in motion my own openness to rewriting and recreating my own scripts and finding my true vocation.

The first act was Colette's story as a young woman, the trials of her love life, the beauty of her relationship with her mother, her intense love of nature and anything sensual. I could play her well at that stage of my life. In fact, when I first read her writing, it connected so deeply with me that it was as if I might have written the words myself, they felt so true to me.

The second act was an adaptation of her novel *Chèri*, in which I played the lead of the story, Lèa, clearly a character autobiographically grown from Colette herself.

But the third act was Colette as an aging woman, struggling to write or not to write. I did my best to do this wise old soul justice, but alas, I was a young woman of twenty-one. A year later, while still in college, Dennis Zacek asked me to re-adapt the production into a one-woman show and perform it at his theatre, Victory Gardens. I played her agelessly, feeling so privileged to speak her poetic candor. Every night, before I would begin the performance, I would spread my arms wide, look at the sky, and say, "Colette, come to me."

And she always did.

I really miss Colette. I think that as I move through these final Acts of my life, she still has much to teach me that I wasn't fully able to understand in my youth. She was an actor in her early life, but knew that her true vocation was to be a writer, a sharer of stories, sensory awakenings, and giver of truths. I like to imagine she and I having tea together today, as she advises me how to age with grace, and still be expressive to the very end.

Colette grew old, her hands were riddled with arthritis, and she stopped writing for a time. She argued with herself about the loss of this expression. She took up embroidery instead. After all writing is a kind of sewing, weaving together ideas and feelings into a tapestry. In her memoir, *Earthly Paradise*, she writes, *"To write, to be able to write. What does it mean? It means spending long hours dreaming before a white page, scribbling unconsciously, letting your pen play around a blot of ink or nibble at a half-formed word...Ah to write...it is but the itching of an old scar."*

Though I mostly use a computer to write, I know what she means, this waiting for divine inspiration to descend. And I also understand that we leave things behind, dreams and the like, and the wounds of those losses grow over into scars, and occasionally they itch, to remind us what we were, what we have become, and what we are still becoming.

When I was presenting at a conference in Paris, my husband and son and I traveled to her birth place, Saint-Sauveur-en-Puisaye, where there was a museum dedicated to her and her life. "En attendant de nous revoir, Colette. Until we meet again," I said, standing in a field of wildflowers outside the museum.

At the end of Earthly Paradise, she writes, "*All my life I have gone to a great deal of trouble for strangers. This is because as they read my work they suddenly found they loved me, and sometimes told me so.*"

I hadn't learned the Enneagram at the time I spoke these words onstage, but each time I uttered them I choked up. I imagine that Colette was a heart type, like me, her secret being the doubt of her worth, and she spent her lifetime, in all her many forms of expression, trying to prove her secret, painful belief wrong. She continues, "*Obviously I am not counting on my tapestry work to win their hearts from now on... How difficult it is to set a limit to oneself... But if all I need to do is try, then all is well; I'm trying.*"

Yes, Colette. How difficult it is to set a limit to oneself. We strive and strive to unlearn our ego structure and see something beyond our imprinted beliefs about who we think we are.

She continues:

Along an echoing road, beating in time at first, then out of time, then coming together again, can be heard the trotting hoofs of two horses in double harness. Controlled by the same hand, the pen and the needle, the habit of work and the wise desire to put an end to it make friends with one another, part, and then are reconciled... Oh, my slow coursers, try to pull together: I can see the end of the road from here.

I don't know how long it was after she wrote this that she passed on and took her final bow. I hope that she still had many years ahead. What is clear is that she never stopped her self-examination, and her quest to make friends with all the parts of herself. That was the end of the road, reconciling her parts, thus her greatest intention realized.

In a satisfying story the character must grow and undergo a real change. Whether they can fully realize the change is unimportant. Transforming need not be complete to be valuable. What is most important is that the character sees themselves clearly, their misguided beliefs about who they *thought* they were recognized as but a role they were cast to play. When a character, or any of us, can embrace for even a moment the truth of who we *really* are, beyond our egoic structure, our delusions, beyond all our roles and masks, we can finally connect with the infinite spark of precious being.

Each Enneagram style has their own epiphany to discover, if they can. The Gut/power types are called to learn that vulnerability is strength, just the other side of the same coin. The light goes on for them that their power lies within, and it was given to them when they were born as a light to shine, and not something they can earn or demand from others. The Heart/worth types are called to learn that their worth is not dependent on proving it. It is a given with each breath they take. It is their birthright. The Head/security types are called to learn that complete security is an illusion in this life of ours, and yet we can feel safe within, feel that we have been given everything we need to live our unique Hero's Journey, whatever the discomforts and challenges. The support we crave is there in each moment in all kinds of ways.

I want to give you a final gift. The following mantras point our Enneagram types in the direction of a profound change that can free us from the limiting roles we have cast ourselves in. These mantras can set into motion a rewrite of the initial script of each type. These mantras can re-center our Enneagram habitual stance and help us play out the scenes of our lives differently. All the mantras are helpful to all of us, because as I have said, all nine types live within us, in our Oneness. You will find them extremely valuable.

"In the pause, life begins." Pause before entering and pause before exiting. In the pause is when you speak the mantra.

#1

I hold life more lightly, finding ease, and compassionately value life's complexity. I see human perfection in imperfection. I see rich possibilities in things just as they are.

#2

The world is my mirror, with its beauty and frailties. I accept I am all of it, dark and light, lovingly. Receiving and giving are one.

#3

From a place of just being, with an open heart, I breathe in life and love, breathe out the same. I am enough and so is everybody else.

#4

I share love freely and generously because my heart is full. Nothing is missing in this moment. I am always connected because everyone is me.

#5

I see my available resources everywhere. They are within me and surround me. I am not separate from anything or anyone. Everything I need is already here.

#6

I trust that all is unfolding as it must. When I listen deeply to my intuition and take action from the place of my inner knowing I am certain I will always find my way home.

#7

I am peaceful, still, and find the greatest adventure is within me. I am long, wide, and deep. I prefer this moment, with all its polarities, exactly as it is.

#8

I embrace that I am human and that my true strength is experienced in cooperation, collaboration, and co-creation with others and the Universe. When I lead I follow, and when I follow I lead.

#9

I see myself and allow my true self to be seen by others. I dismiss nothing and perceive the gold in everything. I say yes, no, or maybe in a clear, strong, and knowing voice.

Final Bows

In the chapter "What Do You Really, Really Want?" I point out that the way to live intentionally is to ask yourself before entering, "What gift can I give myself?"

I realize that one of the important gifts I have given myself was to write this book. I have no idea if it will make any sense to anyone else, or if it will teach you anything you don't already know. What I do know is that the techniques I share in this book have helped many people that I have had the honor to guide as they have done their own personal work.

But most of all, the book has given me a template for myself to live by. It is said that we teach what we need to learn.

When my parents were alive, we would go to the Chicago Botanical Gardens on Rosh Hashanah and Yom Kippur (the Jewish High Holidays) and have times of reflection together. Surrounded by nature, water, earth, and sky, we were in the most sacred of temples. My parents, my husband, my son, and I would read meditations and poetry aloud from diverse spiritual sources, and take the time to evaluate our own growth from the last year, and the things about ourselves we had wanted to change but were still working on.

We took the time to appreciate each other, to ask forgiveness for our insensitivities, and to set new intentions for our relationships with each other for the year ahead. These were dear and profound yearly gatherings. My late parents have now moved on to their next adventures, my son lives in China and is navigating his own Hero's Journey, but my husband and I continue this blessed ritual.

There was a favorite anonymous meditation that we read each year from The New Union Prayer Book, called *On Turning*:

"Now is the time for turning. The leaves are beginning to turn from green to red and orange. The birds are beginning to turn and are heading once more toward the South. The animals are beginning to turn to storing their food for the winter. For leaves, birds, and animals turning comes instinctively. But for us, turning does not come so easily. It takes an act of will for us to make a turn. It means breaking with old habits. It means admitting that we have been wrong; and this is never easy. It means losing face; it means starting all over again; and this is always painful. It means saying I am sorry. It means recognizing that we have the ability to change. These things are terribly hard to do. But unless we turn, we will be trapped forever in yesterday's ways."

In this book we invite lots of turning. We invite ourselves to turn toward the pause before entering or exiting a scene in our lives, and possibly to pause many times during the scenes. We invite turning toward creating an intention for the highest good for all concerned. We invite turning toward greater awareness from all three of our centers of intelligence: head, heart, and body.

We invite turning toward a mirror and acknowledging the roles we play, the masks we wear, and what is underneath them. We invite turning toward empathy, and realizing that our scene partners play different roles with us, but have the very same essence within them as we do. We invite turning toward recognizing the obstacles both outside of ourselves and within ourselves. We invite turning toward seeing our patterns of thinking, feeling, and behaving and examining whether there are other ways to play the scenes of our life more effectively. We are challenging our thoughts, allowing our feelings, and modifying our reactivities. We invite turning towards a rewrite of our narrative, one that includes the claiming of empowerment, worth, and confidence.

Both my friend Art and my father Bernie turned toward these things when it might have been easier to turn away from them. And so, at the end of their Hero's Journeys and their very own plays, after they had completed their last dialogues, made their last gestures, and breathed their last breaths, they both had earned the right to meet their own audience face to face with dignity and pride. Even the angels were applauding.

The end of the run of a play is bittersweet. The actor and the character will not be spending intimate time together anymore, though the actor has been forever changed from the relationship. The world of the play has ended this incarnation. This alchemy of players, whether in foreground or background, must say farewell. If each has played their roles and scenes well, consciously, kindly and carefully, there will be a sense of completion and wholeness, and there will be a readiness to move on.

In real life my dad felt his sense of completion because for him his personal task was to learn how to love and feel loved, and he achieved that. For my friend Art, I believe it was knowing he had lived his life with pure integrity and that he positively impacted so many by doing so. For me, it will be completing the task of knowing that my worth is not something I need to earn, or prove, but that it rests in the mere fact that I was given this precious gift of life.

For you, my dear reader, only you can decide what will ultimately bring you a sense of fulfillment with no regrets. I hope you can gather into yourself some of the resources this book offers: merging the art form of the actor, the insights of the Enneagram, other psycho-spiritual wisdom, the help of your own life-long cast of characters (both dark and light teachers) and your unique audience.

And when you complete your Hero's Journey may you distinctly hear the ovation of this audience, whether it be from a spiritual space, your own observer-witness self, or otherwise.

And may you feel that you can take an honest, unapologetic bow for a well-lived life.

OTHER SCRIPTS OF IMPORTANCE

Earthly Paradise by Colette

Consolations by David Whyte

Sensory Awareness Foundation for trainings
https://sensoryawareness.org/

Anger by Thich Nhat Hanh

You Are Here by Thich Nhat Hanh

The Places That Scare You by Pema Chodron

The Power of Now by Eckhart Tolle

Stillness Speaks by Eckhart Tolle

Point Zero: Creativity Without Limits by Michelle Cassou

Transforming Your Dragons by Jose Stevens

Impro by Keith Johnstone

The I Ching or Book of Changes by Brian Browne Walker

The Body Mind Workbook by Debbie Shapiro

The Enneagram Movie and Video Guide by Thomas Condon

Nine Lenses on the World by Jerome Wagner, PhD

The Enneagram of Death by Elizabeth Wagele

The Wisdom of the Enneagram by Don Richard Riso and Russ Hudson

Beyond the Bookclub: We are the Books we must Read by Ruthie Landis (*also view videos on the Enneagram at* www.ruthienergy.com *or Ruthie's YouTube Channel at* http://bit.ly/ruthie-energy-youtube

ABOUT THE AUTHOR

Photo by Mark Brown Photography

Ruthie Landis believes life is an opportunity to learn and grow. She believes we are all teachers and all students. And she believes we are all actors in the big play of our lives and that in that in our lives we play many roles. In her personal life she began as daughter, granddaughter and sister, then became friend, wife, and mother.

In her professional life her roles continue to be diverse. She is a best-selling author, body-centered psychotherapist and coach, certified hypnotherapist, Enneagram teacher, Award winning international workshop designer, trainer, and facilitator, visual artist, actress, director, acting and presence development coach, Spiritual guide, and Reiki master.

Ruthie uses Nature, Ritual and Ceremony, life transition directed interior design, and the Chinese Five Element theory. It is her mission to reclaim our wholeness with gentle, insight- driven change. Her intention is to bring all these interests and skills together to co-create unique encounters of waking up, self-empowerment, and healing.

For more information, visit www.ruthienergy.com.